A Conspiracy of Silence:

The Murder of Solicitor General Floyd Hoard

"The truth shall always conquer evil to make us free."

—Floyd "Fuzzy" Hoard, 1958

Dedications

This book is dedicated first to the family of Floyd "Fuzzy" Hoard — widow Imogene and children Peggy Jean, Richard, Claudine and Vivian. In the wake of Hoard's murder, his family members remained strong and resilient despite their own personal pain. Over the years, they have kept alive the memory of their husband and father so that their own children and the larger community would never forget the sacrifice he made.

This book is also dedicated to former Georgia Bureau of Investigation Agent Ronnie Angel. When you talk to the few remaining people who were involved in the Hoard case, everyone mentions Ronnie Angel and the tireless work he did in tracking down Hoard's killers.

Finally, this book is dedicated to the man who finally finished the work that Floyd Hoard had begun. Former Jackson County Sheriff Stan Evans took office on January 1, 1985, as the youngest sheriff in the state. He had run against a strong incumbent on a pledge to clean up the county's remaining bootleggers. After taking office, Sheriff Evans completed that pledge at much personal peril to himself.

A Conspiracy of Silence:

The murder of Solicitor General Floyd Hoard

By Mike Buffington
Edited By Alex Pace

Copyright 2018 Mainstreet Newspapers, Inc.

ISBN: 978-1719048187

Published by
Mainstreet Newspapers, Inc.
33 Lee Street
Jefferson, Ga. 30549

Printed by CreateSpace, an Amazon.com company

Available from Amazon.com and other bookstores

First Printing 2018

Foreword

The bombing assassination of solicitor general Floyd "Fuzzy" Hoard of Georgia's Piedmont Judicial Circuit on Aug. 7, 1967, shook the community to its core. The murder happened in Jackson County, one of the three counties that make up the circuit, along with Barrow and Banks counties.

But that tragic event didn't happen in a vacuum. It was the result of decades of lawlessness and corruption which had infected both the social order and public officials in Jackson County.

In the end, five men were convicted of that crime. But in reality, the entire community was complicit. Everyone knew about the wide-open bootlegging and car theft rings in the area. Everyone knew that some local public officials turned a blind eye to the crimes, either because they didn't care, or were corrupt themselves.

Hoard wasn't the first local lawman killed by bootleggers in the Piedmont Judicial Circuit. A marshal had been killed in the small community of Center in Jackson County in 1922 and a federal agent was gunned down at an illegal moonshine still in Banks County in 1947. Yet for decades, juries of local citizens had balked at cracking down on the lawlessness and public corruption. Those who did speak out were often threatened. Fear and intimidation ruled. That only began to change after Hoard's murder.

This book is based on a series of newspaper articles published by *Mainstreet Newspapers* in August 2017 on the 50th anniversary of Hoard's murder. New material has been added here to give more context to the history and environment that led up to the murder. And since those articles were published, more people have come forward with new information that helps give a more complete picture of that era.

Mike Buffington

Contents

Introduction

In the 1950s and 1960s, Northeast Georgia was a hotbed of open criminal activity and public corruption. Rural Jackson County in the northern Piedmont region of the state was especially known for its bootlegging, car theft rings and corrupt public officials. In 1959, a state-ordered county audit implicated a number of Jackson County's elected leaders in a corruption scandal, including law enforcement and judicial officials. In 1960, the county's Superior Court judge was indicted. He and a local lawyer were later disbarred for their role in public corruption. In 1963, Jackson County's sheriff was arrested and convicted for car theft. His successor would also be driven from office and accused of corruption. And the area's extensive bootlegging had grown by the mid-1960s, much of it under the direction of "kingpin" bootlegger A. C. "Cliff" Park.

"It was a 'wild west' show back in the 1960s," recalled former Georgia Bureau of Investigation agent Ronnie Angel about Jackson County's atmosphere of lawlessness.

Jackson County wasn't alone with its "rackets" reputation. Just to the north, the rugged mountain counties of North Georgia were home to thousands of moonshine operations. In fact, lawlessness that revolved around bootlegging, gambling, prostitution and car thefts was rampant in a lot of hamlets all across the South in the 1950s-1980s. Phenix City, Ala., just across the Georgia line, was notorious for its organized crime. An Alabama attorney general who ran on a platform to clean up the town was murdered there in 1954. In August 1967, Pauline Pusser, wife of crusading sheriff Buford Pusser in McNairy County, Tenn., was slain in an ambush by the State Line Mob that ruled the area. That killing was a central part of the 1973 movie, "Walking Tall." And Biloxi, Miss., was a hotbed for gambling and other rackets that lasted for decades. That didn't start to change until after the 1987 murder of a judge and his wife by the local mob.

The common thread in these events was that it took a high-profile murder before the corruption began to be cleaned up. For Jackson County, that was the bombing assassination of Solicitor General Floyd "Fuzzy" Hoard on August 7, 1967.

Major Players

Floyd "Fuzzy" Hoard — Solicitor General who was murdered in Jackson County Ga. in 1967.

A. C. "Cliff" Park — The "kingpin" bootlegger who was convicted of paying for Hoard's murder.

Doug Pinion, George Worley, Lloyd Seay and John Blackwell — Four men convicted along with Park in the murder.

Sheriff L. G. "Snuffy" Perry — Jackson County Ga. sheriff at the time of Hoard's murder who resigned under pressure for having been associated with Park.

Ronnie Angel — The Georgia Bureau of Investigation agent who had worked with Hoard and who later led the probe into Hoard's murder.

Wesley Channell — The Winder, Ga. lawyer appointed to fill Hoard's seat after the murder and who helped prosecute those responsible for the killing.

Luther Hames — A visiting prosecutor from Cobb County Ga. who helped prosecute the murder case.

Judge Mark Dunahoo — Elected at the same time as Hoard in 1964 on a "clean-up" campaign and later presided over the trials of those responsible for Hoard's murder.

Judge Maylon Clinkscales — A Jackson County Superior Court Judge disbarred in 1961 following an audit of the Jackson County government finances.

Sheriff John B. Brooks — Jackson County sheriff from 1943-1964 who was convicted in 1963 on car theft charges.

Tom Williams — Editor of *The Jackson Herald*, the local weekly newspaper, during the 1950s. Williams launched a crusade against the county's bootlegging establishment during his tenure as editor.

Timeline

1875
- First reported raid of a moonshine still in Jackson County.
- Liquor sales banned by state legislation within two miles of Harmony Grove Academy in the county.

1881
- Liquor sales banned in the Newtown District of Jackson County by legislation.

1887
- Jackson County voters enact a county-wide prohibition on the selling of liquor.

1900
- Jackson County voters ban the making of liquor in the county.

1907
- Georgia bans the sale of liquor statewide.

1910
- Bootleggers known as "blind tigers" blow up three homes in the town of Statham in response to the town's prosecution against their businesses.

1915
- A shootout between law enforcement and moonshiners takes place near Statham with two moonshiners injured.

1917
- Georgia passes the "bone-dry" anti-booze law and begins a crackdown against moonshiners.

1920
- National Prohibition enacted.

1922
- The town marshal in the community of Center is killed by suspected moonshiners.

1930
- The Jackson County grand jury calls for a crackdown on bootlegging and lawlessness.

1933
- National Prohibition ends, but Georgia's prohibition remains.

1935
- Georgia votes "wet" for beer and wine, but Jackson County remains "dry."

1940s
- Town of Arcade approves the sale of beer and wine.
- NASCAR is born and largely comes from the moonshine runners in North Georgia.
- Jackson County bootlegger A. C. "Cliff" Park is robbed by a gang associated

with Roy Hall, one of the early auto racers out of Dawson County.
- A federal marshal is killed at a moonshine still just across the Jackson County line in Banks County.

1952
- Floyd Hoard moves to Jackson County.

1953
- Newspaper editor Tom Williams begins a crusade against Jackson County bootlegging.

1955
- Hoard begins practicing law in the town of Jefferson with his father-in-law.

1956
- Hoard and another lawyer are appointed to represent a man accused in a sensational murder case in which a Jefferson merchant was murdered.

1958
- The man convicted and sentenced to death for that 1956 murder is set free after another man confesses to the crime, a story that makes national headlines and brings Hoard widespread recognition.

1959
- A state-mandated audit of the Jackson County government uncovers widespread fraud and public corruption.

1961
- Jackson County Judge Maylon Clinkscales is disbarred for corruption.

1962
- Park is sent for a year to federal prison for selling moonshine.
- Car thefts begin in Jackson County.

1963
- A large car-theft operation is uncovered in Commerce.
- Sheriff John B. Brooks is convicted on car theft charges.

1964
- Hoard is elected Solicitor General of the Piedmont Judicial Circuit and begins a crackdown on bootleggers and car thieves.

1967
- In May, Hoard raids Cliff Park's bootlegging operation, confiscating over $21,000 of booze.
- August 7, Hoard is killed when 10 sticks of dynamite blow up his car.

1968
- Five men, one of whom is Park, are found guilty of conspiring to kill Hoard.

1.

Whiskey Roots Run Deep

Liquor has a long and controversial history in the United States. In 1791, Congress put a tax on whiskey, which ultimately led to the Whiskey Rebellion of 1794 in Western Pennsylvania. George Washington led 13,000 troops to that frontier to put down the rebellion, which was led by farmers who refused to pay the tax. Taxes on liquor later helped fund the Civil War for the Union and alcohol taxes never went away after that.

In the Appalachian Mountains, moonshining became a widespread cottage industry among its Scots-Irish settlers who brought distilling to America from the "old country." Some of that was to fill demand, but it was also a way for independent farmers to show their disdain for government by avoiding alcohol taxes with their illegal stills. That tradition of independence and moonshining spilled out of the mountains and into the Piedmont region of Northeast Georgia.

Jackson County Georgia was created in 1796 and lies just below the foothills of the North Georgia Blue Ridge Mountains. Settlers had been in the area since 1784, and many had been given land grants for their service in the American Revolution. The little town of Jefferson, the county seat, was incorporated in the early 1800s. The county was large geographically and dotted with dozens of small communities whose fortunes rose and fell according to cotton prices and agriculture in general. For most of its history, the community had few large businesses outside of agriculture. By 1920, there were 10 incorporated small towns in the county.

For many decades after its founding, the area was rough and wild. In the

1

early 1800s, a census worker asked for additional pay because Jackson County was so difficult to traverse. During the Civil War, Jackson County was so remote that no battles were fought there. With no coastline, no navigable rivers, no industry and no railroad lines, the area remained a rural backwoods of the state for its first 100 years. Even the addition of railroad lines in the 1870s didn't do much to alter the area's poor economic standing. According to newspapers of the time, the people of Jackson County were defined by the slur "Crackers," poor whites who eked out a living mostly from subsistence farming.

After 1910, the county's population went into decline, a movement that would last for the next 50 years. The boll weevil in the 1920s and Great Depression of the 1930s kept much of the county poor well into the 20th Century. And like in many poor, rural areas of the state, liquor was a common product in Jackson County. Some of that came from legal distilleries in the 1800s, but a lot flowed from moonshine stills hidden in the woods and old barns across the area.

During the late 1800s, a prohibition movement gained steam across the nation. The temperance movement had existed for many decades in Georgia. The earliest anti-liquor temperance society in the state may have even been founded in Jackson County. An 1886 letter published in the *Christian Index* claims that members of Walnut Fork Baptist Church in Jackson County organized the first such group in July 1824. It was known as the "Jackson County Anti-Intemperance Society," according to the letter, which was written by the son of one of the group's founders. But others disputed that, saying the founding of the first temperance society in the state wasn't until 1828 in the town of Milledgeville.

Whatever the truth, the temperance movement didn't get much traction until the late 1800s when communities began to ban liquor sales by having local legislation passed. Often, this would be legislation designed to ban liquor sales within two or three miles of a church or school. In 1875, liquor was banned within two miles of Harmony Grove Academy in Jackson County by legislative action. Another early local legislative act of prohibition was in the Newtown (Nicholson) District of Jackson County in August 1881. The vote was 145 to 45 in favor of a prohibition against selling liquor in that rural district.

The earliest mention of a raid on an illegal moonshine still in Jackson County was in March 1875. According to a newspaper article of the time, two lawmen "dropped into Jackson County by candle light on Monday, and captured a blockade distillery, fifty gallons of whiskey, five hogs and four prisoners..."

In 1885, the State of Georgia began to allow counties to individually hold referendums to ban the sale of liquor. In early 1887, a strong Jackson County prohibition movement organized clubs that were reportedly spread throughout the community to push for a county-wide ban under that law. In March 1887, Jackson County citizens voted to enact a county-wide prohibition. That act even shut down legal liquor sellers who had what was called a "quart license" when the ban went into effect on April 1, 1887.

Jackson County wasn't alone in the prohibition movement in Northeast Georgia. Many of the other area counties also enacted laws against selling booze — except for neighboring Madison County. An 1887 newspaper article said area bar and saloon owners were packing their booze to set up shop in the "Free State of Madison" where liquor sales remained legal.

The prohibition against selling liquor in Jackson County didn't stop the making of moonshine. A raid at Christmas in 1895 captured a still and four men. In 1898, officers raided a large still that had been built underground in Jackson County. The site had been sodded over and it took the law officers some time before they found an entrance where a ladder led down to a 90-gallon copper still and 400 gallons of "beer," the fermented liquid extracted from the mash to be distilled into moonshine. Moonshiner Joe Allen was captured. On their way back from that raid, the revenue officers captured a White County man headed for Jefferson hauling 30 gallons of corn whiskey in a wagon pulled by two mules.

By 1900, the prohibition movement was not only targeting the sale of liquor, but also the making of booze. To that end, the Pendergrass Temperance Union organized a campaign against the manufacturing of liquor in Jackson County. In August 1900, the movement won passage, by 197 votes, to prohibit the manufacture of liquors in the community. At the time, there was only one legal distillery in Jackson County, which was run by G. S. Duke near Pendergrass.

But the county's prohibition on the making and selling of liquor didn't curtail the moonshine industry. In 1905, Green H. Arnold was sentenced to a year in the Jackson County chain-gang for illegally selling liquor. But after serving seven months, he got a pardon from the governor stemming from an unusual event. Two of the Jackson County chain-gang guards had gotten into a fight and one shot the other, then ran away. It was dark and Arnold used a knife to keep 25 chain-gang prisoners from escaping — in the darkness, they thought he was holding a pistol, not a knife. Arnold vowed to give up the liquor business and was released on an order from the governor.

In 1907, the Georgia Legislature, under the lead of Jackson County Senator L. G. Hardman, voted to enact a statewide prohibition on the sale of liquor as of January 1, 1908. One part of that law allowed druggists to furnish alcohol for medicinal purposes, but only one person applied for medicinal liquor in Jackson County between 1908 and 1911.

Overall, the 1907 prohibition law had little effect on the illegal manufacturing and sale of spirits statewide and in Hardman's home county. Illegal booze joints known as "blind tigers" operated everywhere. In 1910, the illegal booze community sent a message to those who wanted to shut them down in the town of Statham, which at the time was in Jackson County (it's now in Barrow County). The town had prosecuted 20 "blind tiger" cases in the summer of 1910. In September, the blind tigers dynamited the homes of the mayor, the town marshal and one of the witnesses involved in the town's summer prosecutions. No one was injured and no arrests were made.

Despite state efforts to stop the manufacturing and sale of liquor between 1907 and 1920, the industry only grew during those years in Northeast Georgia. In the March 1915 term of Federal Court in Athens, some 54 cases were heard against moonshiners and bootleggers in the area. Most were in the mountain counties (Rabun, Habersham and White), but four cases from Jackson County were also on the docket.

In 1915, a shootout between revenue agents and moonshiners in neighboring Barrow County on the Jackson County line near the town of Statham showed just how dangerous the illicit business could be. Three revenue agents waited for hours in the woods in November 1915 and watched as four moonshiners made their brew. At some point, the moonshiners heard the agents and began shooting. A "volley after volley" was fired between the agents and moonshiners, with two of the latter wounded.

Violent incidents weren't just between law enforcement and moonshiners. Sometimes, moonshiners fought against each other. In 1915, two Jackson County moonshiners, J. S. Black and J. H. McIntyre, both age 65, got into a dispute over allegations that Black had stolen some corn whiskey from McIntyre. McIntyre took out warrants for theft against Black. Black was upset when he heard about the warrants and he and some "companions" went to confront McIntyre. Black reportedly went into McIntyre's house, took a gun off a wall rack and threatened to shoot McIntyre if he had indeed taken out warrants. In a bid to save his life, McIntyre denied he had taken out warrants, but as the two sides argued, a court bailiff showed up with the warrants in hand. According to a newspaper report, "the altercation grew lively and hammers, pocket knives and guns were in play." The McIntyre clan later took out warrants against Black for assault. He was found guilty and fined $50.

Although there was violence, some of the law enforcement raids of the era were not without humor. In one 1914 case, federal agents raided the home of George Wilson in Jackson County where they found one gallon of moonshine hidden in a bed. The agents went to Wilson's barn, where they found a 12-gallon keg of moonshine, but while they were gone from the main house, Wilson and an accomplice, Memphis McDaniel, hooked up a buggy with a "fast mule" and sped away with the one-gallon of hooch. Officers eventually caught up to Wilson and McDaniel, but they didn't find the gallon of liquor the two had absconded with.

In another incident in neighboring Banks County in 1921, revenue officers raided a still, but left some of the booze behind. A cow wandered in, drank the liquor, got drunk and "fell off a high place and broke her neck."

In 1917, Georgia passed another law, known as the "bone-dry law," trying to stop the flow of moonshine. State and federal agencies added law enforcement officials to aggressively pursue the moonshine business across the state under the new law. One article stated that in the fiscal year ending in July 1918, some 801 stills had been destroyed in the state due to the increased efforts. Part of the problem, however, was that while state and federal agents were busting stills, not all local law enforcement officials were willing to help. As that article stated, "the officers in some of the counties are in thorough sympathy with the law-breakers."

It doesn't appear that local Jackson County officers were too sympathetic to the moonshine business during that era. In March 1918, Jackson County Sheriff C. D. "Cliff" Barber and two deputies raided a still in the Miller's District and arrested two men, W. M. Davis and Bud Montgomery. They confiscated 300 gallons of "beer" and 20 gallons of "singlings," the first run through a still. They destroyed a 25-gallon copper still. Two months later, Sheriff Barber raided a 45-gallon still in the town of Nicholson and destroyed 600 gallons of beer.

But raiding stills was just part of the crackdown. Officers also chased down those hauling the finished product. In May 1918, Sheriff Barber and a deputy chased a car loaded with 75 gallons of moonshine up Washington Street in Jefferson. After they were caught, the local judge ordered the sheriff to pour the liquor out on Jefferson's public square. As Barber followed the judge's order, a large crowd gathered. According to a newspaper article, some men bent down and attempted to "suck it up from the ground; others lifted it to their mouths with their hands."

In 1919, Jefferson officials captured a wagon loaded with 90 gallons of whiskey after it moved slowly through town, drawn by two mules. The liquor was hidden under a stack of Irish potatoes. The two men captured said they were hauling the booze to someone who had agreed to pay them $12 per gallon. The wagon, mules, booze and potatoes were confiscated to be sold off and the profits divided among city law officers and county officials for their offices. Fines for violating the liquor laws weren't small, either. During that era, violators were fined from $75-$250 in the local courts. That was no small amount in 1919 dollars.

2.
Prohibition Does Little
To Stop Moonshining

The imposition of National Prohibition in 1920 did little to stem the flow of illegal booze in Jackson County and Northeast Georgia as local names continued to show up in federal court cases related to moonshining. The county's main crop, cotton, was starting to fade from low prices and the boll weevil. Illegal liquor was perhaps one of few cash crops left for local farmers. By that time, the moonshine being made in the county wasn't just for local consumption. Prohibition had killed the legal beer, wine and liquor industries, so moonshining for thirsty urban areas like Atlanta 60 miles away became a profitable business. A moonshiner in North Georgia might sell some of his product locally, but a lot of it was made to be taken to larger towns.

Making moonshine was hard work. First, the "mash" had to be prepared. In the early days, that was done in large wooden boxes where cracked corn was mixed with water, yeast and sometimes sugar.

After it fermented for a few days, the resulting "beer" (the strained liquid from the mash) was put into the still pot (usually made of copper) and heated to around 173 degrees so that the alcohol would evaporate and flow out to a twisting condenser tube called a "worm," which was cooled in a "worm box" where cool water flowed around the "worm" to turn the alcohol vapor into liquid — moonshine. The first run was called "singlings" and that was often run again through the process to distill the alcohol even more, the result being "doublings."

There were various variations on that process — often a "thump keg" containing "beer" was used between the still and the worm box as a filter to raise the alcohol output. But no matter how it was done, it required carrying or lifting heavy sacks of sugar, cornmeal and liquids. And because stills were hidden deep in the woods, most of the lugging of ingredients and finished product had to be carried in and out by hand to avoid detection. The result was that the men who worked on the stills were often younger family members, or people hired by an older still owner.

Sometimes, the results of that process were tainted either by dirty equipment, or cutting the final product with poison. In 1920, a 60-year-old Jefferson man died of typhoid fever and drinking poison whiskey, according to state records.

In 1922, Jackson County had its first law enforcement officer killed by moonshiners. Three men from White County in the North Georgia mountains drove to the small community of Center in southern Jackson County one Sunday morning. Driving a Ford touring car, the three stopped at the Presbyterian Church and created a disturbance.

Center Marshal Fred Crawford, age 35, went to the church to quell the uproar (the men were reportedly drunk and looking for a local woman). According to news articles from that time, Crawford stood on the car's running board as he "escorted" the three to the town jail to make bond. But one of the men hit him over the head with an iron pipe. Crawford fell from the car and died later that day of a fractured skull.

Two of the three men were later caught and officers said they believe the men had been hauling moonshine from White County at the time of the murder.

In 1923, one of Jackson County's largest stills was found two miles south of the town of Hoschton, near the Barrow County line. Two large copper stills and 2,500 gallons of beer were found, with the beer ready to be processed into liquor. Four men were arrested in the raid.

In 1927, officers found the smallest moonshine still ever in the county near Fowler's Mill. Dubbed a "kindergarten distillery," the tiny still was found in a children's play area near another, larger still. The "baby still" could make one quart of liquor. According to a newspaper article, it was used by adults to teach young children how to make moonshine. Clearly, National Prohibition had done nothing to stop the manufacturing of liquor by rural moonshiners. If anything, it had increased the practice.

Federal court records during the 1920s are full of local people charged with possessing or manufacturing moonshine. One Jackson County man found himself in more trouble in federal court in Athens after he was convicted for making liquor. After being found guilty, W. A. Fulcher slipped out of the court-house before the judge could sentence him. He was later caught and told officials that he had borrowed a "team" (horses or mules and a wagon) and had left court to return the team to its owner. He was put in jail for 10 days and fined $150.

By 1930, the open violation of National Prohibition laws and the rise of criminal gangs throughout the country had many people calling for repeal. Locally, the idea of prohibition continued to have support in theory, but apparently not in practice.

The February 1930 Grand Jury of Jackson County reported that there were two communities in the county that "have forcefully brought to the attention of this body some very objectionable conditions existing, comprising the selling of whiskey, excessive drunkenness, operation of houses of ill repute, etc." The grand jury went on to say:

"Citizens complain bitterly, but these same citizens either cannot, or prefer not, to furnish the necessary evidence for indictment. We feel it is the duty of our officers to render some conscientious and diligent service in helping to clean out these objections. We understand our officers have stood ready several times to make raids on certain alleged 'blind tigers' in these communities, but in every instance have been unable to get citizens to swear out the necessary papers. We feel federal officers working with our officers could accomplish the desired results."

That strong statement was clearly designed to pressure local law enforcement to be more aggressive in pursuing the moonshining and "blind tiger" businesses. The other aspect of that statement was to complain that while people talked about the moonshine and bootlegging problem, they were apparently fearful of swearing out warrants or testifying.

But that February 1930 grand jury call had little effect in changing those problems. The next grand jury, meeting in August 1930, said essentially the same thing as its predecessor:

"One certain part of the county has certain persons residing therein that are dealing in whiskey, wholesale and retail. Our body has spent considerable time on this and investigated to the fullest extent of existing conditions and we recommend that the officers of this county give this special attention and that all the good people join in making this a better community."

9

Those two themes — that local law enforcement should be more aggressive against bootleggers and that citizens should be willing to step forward and testify — would be repeated over and over in the coming decades by future grand juries and other community leaders.

But in the 1930s, the grand jury pressure didn't make much difference. Only one moonshine case is listed in the February 1931 Superior Court of Jackson County docket where Dock Carter was fined $50 — lower than the fines of earlier years.

In 1933, the grand jury said that "persons interested in cases investigated by this body" had tried to influence — probably bribe — members of the grand jury. The statement doesn't reveal who or what kinds of cases were involved, but it's not difficult to imagine that the county's bootlegging community was perhaps behind that.

In 1933, National Prohibition ended, but Georgia didn't end its state prohibition until 1935. That year, the state voted to stay dry on liquor, but to allow beer and wine sales. In that 1935 vote, Jackson County citizens voted against legalizing all three — liquor, beer and wine. Only one county precinct, Center, voted "wet," but just by three votes.

Later in 1935, a large group of citizens attended a Jefferson City Council meeting to protest any effort by the city government to grant a beer license in the city. The Jackson County commission chairman was also at that meeting and assured the crowd that the county would not license beer in rural areas, a promise that would be kept for over six decades.

In the 1940s, the small Town of Arcade near Jefferson became the only community to license beer and wine sales in Jackson County. The town would prosper for the next 40 years, becoming the beer capital of Georgia in the 1970s, in large part by selling beer cheaply to students at the nearby University of Georgia in Athens and from supplying area bootleggers with beer to resell.

Arcade's legal sales didn't matter very much in the 1940s. The illegal sale of beer, wine and moonshine continued to be widespread in Jackson County and all of North Georgia even after Arcade made beer and wine legal.

In 1940, another Jackson County grand jury called for action against the illicit booze community. It called on the county board of commissioners to "see that our laws are enforced and if necessary, employ special officers whose special duty shall be to enforce the law in regard to the sale of intoxicants and the operation of road houses."

But nothing happened and the bootleg business continued unmolested.

It was during this era — late 1930s and 1940s — that the moonshining business led to the creation of what has become a national sport. Moonshine runners out of the North Georgia mountains began challenging each other to races in their souped-up moonshine-running cars.

It began as informal contests, but soon gained popularity in the Piedmont region and across the South. Moonshine runners Lloyd Seay and Roy Hall from nearby Dawson County, Ga., were two of the early stars of the sport. By the late 1940s, the auto races were organized and NASCAR was formed.

The sport made moonshiners and moonshine running seem romantic. In his book, *"Real NASCAR, White Lightning, Red Clay,"* author Daniel Pierce says that the fast cars gave the early race car drivers — many of whom were moonshine-runners — an idealized image.

"Liquor runners also took on the status of folk heroes to many children and teens in the region," he observes.

That image of folk hero moonshiners was also reflected in popular culture. The comic strip "Snuffy Smith" became very popular in that era with its exaggerated take on hillbilly culture and Smith's character as a "corn-likker" moonshiner who fought "revenuers."

That wasn't the only pop culture icon to romanticize moonshining in that era. The 1958 movie "Thunder Road" starring Robert Mitcham as a moonshine runner became a cult classic (a Revenue agent is killed in a car bomb planted by a moonshine kingpin in the movie).

But the rough side of the moonshine business remained. In 1947, another area lawman was killed at the hands of moonshiners in the Piedmont Judicial Circuit. Just north of the City of Commerce across the Banks County line, federal agent Melvin "Mell" Clark was gunned down at a moonshine still.

Clark, along with six other state and federal agents, had staked-out the still in the woods about two miles south of the Town of Homer in Banks County. Just before the raid began, shots were fired and Clark was killed, but not before he fired off five shots in return. Three men were seen running away, but the other agents couldn't catch them.

A huge posse was formed as 100-200 farmers — some wearing their overalls according to newspaper reports — gathered with their guns to search the woods for the suspects. Seven area sheriffs set up a command post and bloodhounds were brought in to give chase. It became one of the largest manhunts in the state's history. The search went through the woods of Banks County and into Jackson County for six days and nights. Because there were so many men searching, law enforcement eventually pared the posse down to just 75 men.

The still where Clark was killed was owned by John Lewellen and Doc Crump, both of whom confessed when confronted by law enforcement. They told agents the names of the men who worked for them at the still — three "Negro" brothers, Red, Demorest and Uris Gather.

Federal agent Duff Floyd, who became a legend in North Georgia, and two state agents staked out the brothers' parents' house and began talking to the parents.

In his book *"Mountain Spirits,"* author Joseph Dabney interviewed Floyd later about what happened. Floyd said that the parents were worried about their sons getting shot by some of the posse scouring the woods for them. Floyd assured them he would take care of them if they turned themselves in. A 10-year-old girl was sent into the woods to relay the message, and Demorest and Uris turned themselves in that night. Before taking the brothers to jail in Atlanta, Floyd let them eat supper with their parents since they hadn't eaten anything the previous week while hiding out in the woods.

After their meal, Floyd asked the brothers the fastest backroads to Atlanta and he "drove like fury" to get them safe and away from the large crowd of armed men. Floyd said he only contacted the search headquarters in Commerce after the men were secure in the Atlanta jail. Uris later confessed to the shooting and was sentenced in federal court to life in prison.

Agent Clark, who had been sheriff of Hall County before going to work for the U.S. Treasury Department, left behind a wife and two sons, one of whom was just a week old. (The following year, moonshiner Crump alleged that he had conspired with Banks County Sheriff Farris Brewer and three others in the illegal moonshine business. Sheriff Brewer was tried in federal court in Gainesville in December 1948 and acquitted.)

It was danger like the Clark killing which helped cower local citizens from prosecuting bootleggers. By 1950, local law enforcement and the courts were — if not directly complicit — then certainly not aggressively pursuing the bootlegging business.

The illicit trade had gained political power and influence during the era of Prohibition, the Depression and World War II. After the war, sugar rations ended, allowing moonshiners to ramp up their production again. In addition, men returned home from overseas thirsty. The local bootlegging businesses filled that need and prospered even more than they had during Prohibition. The stage was set for a confrontation.

3.
Bootlegging Gets Pushback

By the early 1950s, the illegal booze business in Jackson County had evolved from its independent moonshiner roots. After Prohibition ended and legal beer, wine and liquor became available, it wasn't necessary to just sell moonshine made by area farmers. Selling beer, wine and "red" whiskey — wholesale and retail — became hugely profitable. The trade had grown beyond just moonshine and was referred to loosely as just "bootlegging," a term from the Midwest that referred to men carrying a flask of liquor in their boots.

Jackson County was in a good geographic location to be a major part of this enterprise. The county was rural enough to hide moonshine stills; it was close to the mountains where moonshine expertise and supplies were available; and it was close to the larger Atlanta, Athens and Gainesville markets. By the end of the 1950s, Jackson County would register more bootlegging cases in the courts than any other county in the state.

That wasn't just isolated individuals doing the bootlegging. By the early 1950s, the illegal booze business had become organized with some larger players funding and supplying smaller sellers, in addition to running moonshine and wholesaling to other locations outside the area. Those operations required relationships with others in the illegal booze business. It became a network with a tight inner circle locally and a looser band of relationships with other nearby bootleggers who could supply the various kinds of booze needed to meet demand. Everybody in the business knew everyone else and a tacit understanding of territory evolved.

All of that led to a need to protect this growing criminal enterprise — and its profits — from law enforcement. Moonshiners could hide their stills in the woods and the runners could disguise their cars loaded with liquor, but hiding public retail bootlegging operations in a dry county wasn't possible. That led bootleggers to start supporting local sheriff candidates and judicial officials who wouldn't be too aggressive in shutting down their illegal houses.

Over time, the illegal booze business became a corrupting and corrosive influence on local officials. In addition, the bootlegging operations in Jackson County learned how to play the legal system to their advantage, often tying the courts into knots and playing one set of judicial officials against another. It was a game and more often than not, the bootleggers won.

Although the rural area of Jackson County was legally "dry," beer, wine and liquor were easily available at any of the many bootlegging houses that dotted the area in the 1950s. The only time bootleggers weren't in business, according to published reports, was when the grand jury was in session.

Jefferson native Gus Johnson, who would later play a key part of the Floyd Hoard investigation, remembers the 1950s as a different era from today:

"It was such a different time," he recalled. "....The KKK was still active. I remember daddy had enough political connections... (so that) he would get word some way that the KKK would be riding that night. So my dad, my uncle Jimmy, myself and a guy who used to work with us doing mechanics, we'd all get weapons, shotguns and rifles, and each stay at the house and at our tenant farmers. It would be a huge number of Ku Klux riding in cars with their hoods on. I don't know whether they knew we were there armed or not, but they never stopped at the farm."

Access to beer and liquor in the 1950s was pretty easy, Johnson said. One time in the mid-1950s, Johnson and some of his fellow Jefferson High School football players got caught after paying a visit to Cliff Park's bootlegging operation in Pendergrass. Johnson, a non-drinker, was the driver:

"I was probably a senior in high school and we had an old '53 Chevrolet station wagon and you could load that thing down (with people). So we must've had seven or eight football players sitting there, probably on a Tuesday night. I was the driver and we went through and got our orders in (at Park's bootlegging house) and rode around ... we wound up parking at the old track field. One of the players was sitting on the hood. The old Chevrolet had a sharp ornament on the hood, so I put the brakes on and he went to

14

sliding off the front and tore his pants. He knew he was in trouble.

"We had a lot of fun that night and obviously word got around. The next morning, we showed up for school and coach (Stooge) Davis was out front waiting on us. He took everybody up to the gym... that wasn't very pleasant with Coach Davis.

"At the time, the grand jury was in session. It wasn't long, probably 2 o'clock, coach Davis called everyone up to the office and we were loaded up and taken to the courthouse. Of course, we made our vows that we didn't know nothing. We didn't buy no beer; we didn't know anything.

"Everybody went in and gave their spiel. I knew probably half or more of the men on the grand jury. It was a little bit hard going in there saying I didn't know anything. They asked, 'But Gus, weren't you driving?'

'Yes, but I'm not sure where we went.'

"One of them (grand jury members) got up and went out to a pay phone and called my dad. Probably in 30 minutes, he was up there. My memory got better pretty quick. I had to be the 'rat' I guess to tell where we got the beer. I didn't have a whole lot of choice. Looking back, that was right funny.

"I don't remember anything being done. I'm sure with that case it just sort of disappeared."

For a time in the 1950s, there was a vocal public backlash against the boot-legging operations. That was due to a new local newspaper editor and publisher, Tom Williams, who leased *The Jackson Herald* in August 1950 from owner John Holder, who had run the paper for the previous 59 years.

Holder had been more of a politician than an editor, running for governor four times, heading the state department of transportation and holding the Speaker of the House's position for a number of years. Holder was anti-booze during Prohibition, but he didn't do much reporting about the illegal liquor business in the county. When Holder did write about local court sessions, it was usually to flatter lawyers and judges who were his friends.

Williams was a different kind of editor. As an outsider, he didn't have many local ties or qualms about reporting what was really going on. He reported on actual court proceedings — naming names and listing results.

By 1953, Williams began a crusade against bootlegging in Jackson County, a crusade he would continue until he left the paper in 1959. One aspect of Williams' crusade was to focus attention on how the local legal system dealt with bootlegging cases. Jackson County had, and still has, two local courts — Superior Court and City Court. (City Court was eventually renamed State Court.)

The City Court, created in 1892, has long been controversial. It was created as a successor to older, rural Inferior Courts that dealt with misdemeanors and small civil cases. But almost from the start, county grand juries and other political leaders called for the City Court to be fixed or abolished, a sentiment that lasted into the 1990s. It was considered — at best — as being redundant to Superior Court, or at worst, ineffective and corrupt.

Over the decades, illegal alcohol cases made in Jackson County by local law enforcement bounced between the Superior Court and the City Court. Cases made by federal agents usually landed in Federal Court. So a bootlegging case could end up in any one of three different court systems, depending on the charges, the size of the bust and what law enforcement agency made the charges.

In 1951, the Jackson County Grand Jury made a strong call for doing away with the City Court, saying its "fines and punishments are entirely too small in a great proportion of cases and not in keeping with the seriousness of the offense."

That grand jury concluded its remarks by saying:

"In lieu of this City Court, we recommend that handling of this Court's cases in the Superior Court by two additional terms, or in any satisfactory manner the Superior Court should work out."

Nothing happened and the county's City Court would increasingly be used in the coming years by bootlegging defendants as a way to avoid serious punishments.

Problems were also evident in Superior Court. At that same term of court in February 1951, a bootlegger charged with two counts of possessing beer and wine for sale was found not guilty by a jury. Sometimes, jury members were sympathetic to the bootleggers, or perhaps bought off.

In 1953, editor Williams began to focus on the corrupting influence the illegal bootlegging was having on Jackson County's youth. The February 1953 grand jury had called on community leaders to address what it said was a growing problem of juvenile delinquency. Williams echoed that call in an editorial, saying the problem "is the result of a bunch of hoodlums who influence many youngsters without proper supervision to do their dirty work for them. This is from delivering bootleg liquor to crimes of a more serious nature."

Williams said in that editorial he had received a list of names of "about 55 youngsters who were working for or under the 'thrill' influence of Jackson County's most famous hoodlums." Williams said he contacted the parents of those named in the list, finding some of the parents drunk.

"Their bootleg moonshine was provided by the very ring leaders who were leading their sons into more serious crime."

In early November 1953, Williams penned a lengthy editorial calling for an increase in the penalties for those convicted of bootlegging:

"Bootleggers are caught nearly every week. A case may be made; a $300 to $500 security bond posted; the bootlegger is free to continue his illegal business. Often he is caught over and over again between sessions of the Superior Court. Bond is posted again and again."

Williams called for a change in state laws to "deal out more severe penalties for bootlegging." He suggested, among other items, a $5,000 bond and that all cases go to Superior Court.

A letter to the editor that same week echoed this pushback against bootlegging. The letter, which was not signed, said that taxi drivers in Jefferson and Commerce were taking people to bootlegging locations to buy their booze.

"Why don't you look into this and say something?" the letter asked.

A week later, Williams' crusade against local bootleggers got a tragic boost when a Hoschton teenager died after drinking moonshine. Ray Stephenson, 17, and two other boys (ages 16 and 21) bought moonshine from Barrow County bootlegger Herman Dunagan on a Sunday morning and drove to some woods near the old Hoschton hospital where they began drinking from the half-gallon jar.

Stephenson passed out about 45 minutes to an hour later and the other two boys put him in the backseat of their car. They drove around the county for a while and eventually returned to Stephenson's home where they discovered he wasn't breathing. Stephenson's parents were called and they rushed him to the hospital in nearby Winder, but he was already dead. A subsequent investigation found that the moonshine wasn't tainted, but that Stephenson had drunk a large amount and died of alcohol poisoning.

The teen's death galvanized the debate over bootlegging, at least for a time. A letter to the editor in early December 1953 referred to the death: "This death should be a spur to the conscience of every decent, law-abiding citizen..."

The Georgia Legislature responded to the teen's death by passing a bill that made it a felony to sell liquor to a minor. That legislation was co-authored by

Jackson County Rep. Mac Barber.

A month after Stephenson's death, a state revenue agent and two Jackson County deputies raided seven locations in the county and arrested three people for bootlegging. The next week, four moonshine stills were raided, two near Commerce, one at Sandy Creek in South Jackson and the fourth in a poultry house in Pendergrass.

The Pendergrass still was huge. It could produce 250 gallons of moonshine a day and there was 5,000 gallons of mash on hand. Three men, one from Dawsonville, one from Canton and one from Dahlonega, were arrested. That raid was done only by state agents and didn't include any local law officers. Local law enforcement, along with state agents, raided the other three stills, but no one was arrested during those raids.

Also during December 1953, the state posted a full-time revenue agent in Jackson County. Grady Cook came from Florida to the City of Commerce in Jackson County where he would soon crack down on bootlegging in the Northeast Georgia area.

In the first week of the new year, editor Williams outlined a 10-point platform the newspaper planned for 1954, one of which was to expose bootleggers. That point read: "To publicly expose bootleggers and assist in the elimination of their operations in Jackson County."

Williams also called on the upcoming February 1954 grand jury to conduct an investigation into the county's bootlegging operations. The grand jury did reportedly discuss the problem, but rather than pressuring law enforcement to take action, it blamed citizens for not reporting the locations of bootlegging activity and for not taking out warrants against bootleggers.

Said the grand jury:

"It is most disappointing for this Grand Jury to remain in session and open to the public during the greater part of two weeks and see that same citizenry fail their responsibility so completely by not coming forth and filing charges against these law violators..."

Nevertheless, state agent Cook, along with a new associate, I. W. Davis, hit two county stills and confiscated 23 gallons of moonshine in a series of raids during the spring of 1954. On one raid, a county deputy assisted, but as with many previous raids, Sheriff John B. Brooks wasn't part of the bust.

In July 1954, editor Williams called for increased regulation on county taxi cabs. Williams said that the towns of Jefferson and Commerce had 30 taxis, far too many for the small population of the area. The cabs, it seems, had become an important part of the bootlegging distribution system.

"Cabs keep busy carrying customers out to bootleggers where they pick up their moonshine. Recently since a crackdown has been made on bootleggers, the taxis have made arrangements to pick up moonshine at appointed spots near and within the city limits," Williams wrote in an editorial.

The editor called on local governments to limit the number of cabs in the county and to put "rigid qualifications" in place for drivers.

One cab driver was tried for helping bootleggers during the August term of court in 1954, but the judge declared a mistrial. The grand jury also returned indictments on a number of bootlegging cases, but at the August trials, seven of the accused jumped bond.

The raids of late 1953 and early 1954 had raised a lot of hope that the bootlegging business could be crushed, but those charged simply forfeited their bonds, considering it as just the price of doing business.

Still, revenue agents Cook and Davis continued their work, busting another moonshine still in September 1954 on the Maysville Road, about three miles from Jefferson.

In March 1955, state and local agents busted three stills in southern Jackson County off of Hwy. 129 on land that had been used by the University of Georgia as an experiment farm. Later that year in September 1955, the state made a massive moonshine raid in eight Northeast Georgia counties, arresting 171 people and confiscating 48 vehicles, 20 of which were taxi cabs used to distribute moonshine. Five of those taxi cabs were in Jackson County with 14 more out of the neighboring town of Athens. Only one taxi cab was left in Athens after the raids, according to a newspaper article about the raids.

In 1959, a four-county chase of a moonshine "tripper" echoed the 1958 movie, "Thunder Road." Two state agents, along with the sheriff of Banks County, chased Jack Ferguson of nearby Habersham County through the backroads of Banks, Franklin, Madison and Jackson counties at speeds of 120-miles-per-hour. Ferguson was driving a "high-powered" 1957 car hauling 190 gallons of moonshine, according to newspaper reports.

In December 1959, the City of Jefferson, the Jackson County seat, held a referendum on "going wet," a move that would have helped undermine the bootlegging community.

An editorial titled, "Do we stagger to the polls to vote dry," in *The Jackson*

Herald endorsed the idea, saying booze was available illegally anyway.

"It seems that the only possible solution to the question without making hypocrites of us all is to legalize the sale of beer, or quit endorsing the sale of it," the editorial said. But the move to legalize beer sales in Jefferson failed by two votes. (Another vote was held in Jefferson in 1961 and it failed by 35 votes.)

There were some interesting bootlegging court hearings in the late 1950s, too. One case brought to the county's City Court in December 1959 was called a "Perry Mason thriller" in a *The Jackson Herald* article. Defendant Rosco Howington at first didn't appear in court when his case was called. Prosecutor Nat Hancock told the judge he couldn't proceed without the defendant.

Eventually, Howington entered the courtroom, along with three other men who were about his same size and height. All four sat at the defense table. Two witnesses, both undercover agents, testified that they had bought beer and liquor from Howington and pointed him out from the witness stand.

But the defense questioned the reliability of the two and argued it was mistaken identity. The jury was deadlocked and a mistrial was declared. After that, prosecutor Hancock decided to delay calling seven other bootlegging cases that had been scheduled for that term of court.

Both the 1959 editorial endorsing the idea of Jefferson voters approving legal alcohol sales and the 1959 story about the courtroom drama were written by a young Jefferson lawyer named Floyd Hoard.

4.

Corruption Explodes

Many had long suspected that Jackson County's bootleggers had the help of the local law enforcement community and judicial system, if not directly, then indirectly through a lack of interest and action. Many of the raids on moonshine operations and bootleggers throughout the 1950s had been done mostly by state or federal agents. When local authorities were involved, it was usually a deputy — Sheriff John B. Brooks seldom participated in the raids himself.

Many people didn't consider bootlegging too serious in that era. In his book, *"Nothing But the Truth,"* Jackson County attorney James Horace Wood acknowledged that fact:

"This is a common attitude in bootleg country. A whiskey charge isn't considered much more serious than a parking ticket in the lower courts, except that it might cost a few dollars more for the fine."

But in 1958, something unusual happened — a local judge put a target on area bootleggers in a way that had never been done before. In August 1958, Superior Court Judge Maylon Clinkscales ordered a series of raids on local bootleggers. Clinkscales had only taken office as judge in 1957 and had risen to quick prominence by presiding over the trial related to the sensational 1956 murder of Jefferson businessman Charles Drake. Clinkscales' tenure as judge would later prove to be brief and troubled, but for a moment in the summer of 1958, he looked like a crusader against Jackson County's bootleggers.

Following Clinkscales' order, a large group of state and federal agents assembled on Friday, August 1, 1958, and raided bootleggers in Jefferson, Pendergrass and Commerce. They arrested eight people and confiscated a load of illegal booze from the various locations, including from the popular Moose Club in Commerce.

Clinkscales ordered all of the defendants held for 72 hours in jail, without a bond, and to appear in his courtroom Monday morning. That was significant because the grand jury would be in session that Monday. Bootleggers mostly closed down when grand juries were meeting in February and August because if they were caught, they could be taken before the grand jury, indicted, and held for trial. Bootleggers preferred to just post a bond if they were caught and then skip any hearings, forfeiting their bond and avoiding a more serious punishment, such as jail time.

But the bootleggers from those raids wouldn't be held in the jail until Monday as Clinkscales had ordered. On Saturday following the Friday night raids, the county's other court, the City Court, got involved.

Lawyers for the bootleggers served paperwork on Sheriff Brooks, who then contacted City Court solicitor Nat Hancock. Hancock contacted City Court Judge Early Stark, who held a quick hearing on Saturday afternoon. Stark set a $500 bond for each of the eight bootleggers and ordered them released from jail. Sheriff Brooks opened the jail doors and the bootleggers were free.

Judge Clinkscales was furious. When Superior Court opened that Monday, he blasted the City Court and called on the grand jury to back him up.

"I personally gave written orders directing the sheriff and officers to hold these persons in jail until they could be brought before me for a hearing... I have this authority and you (the grand jury) had a right to have them here..."

Clinkscales also said that his Superior Court had ultimate jurisdiction over the cases and that the City Court couldn't overrule that. Then something strange happened. City Court Judge Stark met with the grand jury behind closed doors. When he came out, Clinkscales had lost the fight. The grand jury subsequently refused to indict the eight bootleggers.

Then it went further. In its presentments, the grand jury undercut Clinkscales by saying the City Court should be left alone and should be used to hear most of the county's misdemeanor cases like bootlegging. That is the opposite of what a number of grand juries had said over the previous decades.

That position riled local newspaper editor Tom Williams, who blasted the grand jury and Stark in an editorial over their handling of the matter. City

Court Judge Stark responded by challenging Williams, saying that not one person in the county would protest the grand jury's decision to not indict the bootleggers. Williams then got a petition of 135 names protesting the action and presented it to the grand jury to prove Stark wrong. During all that controversy, the editor got death threats from the bootlegging community.

"Threats made on the life and property of *The Herald* are not new," wrote Williams. "We have had hundreds over the years — just about any time we mention a bootlegger in the news columns or write an editorial against bootlegging."

Clinkscales, upset at Stark having yanked the bootlegging cases away and interfering with the grand jury, issued an injunction to shut the City Court down. That move would eventually be lifted by the State Supreme Court.

Despite his 1958 actions targeted toward bootleggers, it turned out that Clinkscales was not really the anti-bootlegging crusader he appeared to be. In February 1959, a new county grand jury began an investigation into Clinkscales and other county officials over questions about the handling of county funds. When he realized he was a target in the probe, Clinkscales dismissed the grand jury before it finished its work, leading to a huge public outcry.

In a dramatic move, the state Legislature passed a bill a few days later that ordered a complete audit of Jackson County's government, including the courts, for 1957 and 1958.

That 127-page audit was released in May 1959 and it was stunning. Among other items, the audit alleged that the county had purchased over half of its automotive gas from a company Clinkscales owned; that Clinkscales and Winder attorney Marvin Pierce Jr. had schemed to defraud the county of a $2,000 fee on the sale of hospital bonds; that the county government was in bad financial condition due to "negligence on the part of Jackson County administrative officials"; that two county commissioners had been doing business with the county; and that Solicitor General Alfred Quillian and Sheriff Brooks had profited in a scheme where the county "threw away $9,000."

The next grand jury in August 1959 indicted both Clinkscales and Pierce for conspiracy over the hospital bond sale and for barratry against Clinkscales for his having shut down the county's City Court in 1958. Clinkscales' subsequent arrest was the first time a sitting Superior Court judge in Georgia had been placed under arrest. He was released on a $2,000 bond.

Despite the indictment, Clinkscales continued to serve as judge. He was soundly defeated for re-election in September 1960 by Richard B. Russell III of Winder.

In 1961 after leaving office, Clinkscales stood trial for disbarment. The disbarment proceedings were filed by 23 realtors and private citizens of Jackson County on behalf of the state, charging Clinkscales had "within and over the past two years engaged in a course and continuity of action consisting and comprised of acts and deeds of willful, deceitful, unlawful and immoral misconduct in his profession and in both his individual and official capacities."

Among other items, the disbarment petition included allegations that the judge used his power to get Jackson County's oil business for his petroleum distributorship in Commerce and had charged the county inflated prices for gasoline. The disbarment petition also charged that:

• as judge of the Superior Court, Clinkscales had favored attorney Pierce in numerous instances which brought the attorney "unconscionable fees and renumerations." Among the accusations were that for a fee, Clinkscales had released inmates from prison who had been represented by Pierce.

• he used a two-man police force to "serve his personal interest," including the delivery of two cases of bootleg whiskey to his home.

• he attempted to manipulate a grand jury list.

• he had law enforcement raid and close a fraternal club because its manager refused to pay him $10,000 in cash and $500 a month for "protection." (Clinkscales reportedly wanted to run for governor and one witness said he wanted the money to help finance that campaign. In hindsight, his 1958 roundup of bootleggers may have been an attempted shakedown to help fund his political aspirations.)

After three days of questioning 30 witnesses, the prosecution rested its case. When the defense offered no witnesses, the prosecution asked the judge to direct a verdict of guilty.

On Feb. 9, 1961, Clinkscales was disbarred with a directed verdict from Judge F. Fredrick Kennedy of Augusta. The story was the front page headline in the *Atlanta Constitution* the next day.

In October 1961, the same judge issued a directed verdict to disbar attorney Pierce on one count after a Barrow County jury had acquitted him on seven of nine total counts.

A disgraced judge, complicit lawyers and a corrupt county government weren't the only problems in Jackson County in the 1950s and '60s. In 1958, the poll manager of the Minish (Commerce) voting district was convicted of making fraudulent returns in that year's primary elections. The Court of Appeals later overturned that conviction.

Even larger, however, was the corruption that centered around Jackson County Sheriff John B. Brooks.

Brooks was a big, beefy man with a baby face who had first been elected sheriff in 1943 after an incumbent sheriff died in office. His maternal grandfather had been sheriff for a time in Jackson County in the late 1800s and he had a brother who served as a state representative from Jackson County from 1935-1940. Among his hobbies was raising bird dogs for field trial competitions. In 1959, he was president of the Peach State Fox Hunters Association.

Brooks became very popular with his constituents. Former bootlegger Troy Lee Griffith said Brooks was well-liked because he helped people get out of trouble, often by going to City Court Judge Stark and having him take care of a case.

"You'd be surprised at the intelligent people in Jackson County whose kids would get in trouble and they'd go talk to John B. and he'd get them out of it," Griffith said. "That's how (Brooks) got so popular in this county... by helping people."

But Brooks was also deeply involved in the county's bootlegging and criminal underworld. A native of Pendergrass, he was a neighbor to the county's "kingpin" bootlegger, Cliff Park.

Brooks was also into bootlegging himself. One of those who helped Brooks in running whiskey was Griffith, who recalled what happened once when a county deputy caught him with a load of liquor in Braselton:

"I was carrying it over there to Winder. I told Bart (the Jackson County deputy who worked for Brooks), 'y'all don't want to mess with this liquor.' They brought me back to the jailhouse and I had 300 cases on it (the truck.) John B. pulled up and ol' Bart was so proud of hisself — but John B. slapped him all the way across that old (jail) yard up there and told me to take it where I was supposed to carry it."

The liquor belonged to Sheriff Brooks and Griffith was hauling it for him, something the deputy didn't know when he stopped the truck.

By the late 1950s, Brooks began coming under increased pressure from various agencies for his disregard of the law. For one thing, that 1959 county audit uncovered the fact that Brooks and solicitor general Quillian had sold insolvent bonds to the county in 1958. Brooks and Quillian purchased the bonds back for $9,000 and were not indicted.

25

Then there was Brooks' personal tax problems. The *Atlanta Constitution* checked Brooks' property tax records in 1959 and found that he hadn't paid county property taxes for the previous eight years. Not including interest or fees, he owed the county $955 in back taxes.

When the newspaper's reporter asked Brooks about it, he said, "I didn't know I was that far behind. I just hadn't been able to pay them."

Brooks went on to say his not paying property taxes actually helped the county because when he did eventually pay them, the county would earn seven percent interest on what he owed. It's not clear he ever paid the back taxes. At the time, back property taxes were voided after seven years if they hadn't been entered into the county's execution docket, a move that was the responsibility of Brooks and the county tax collector. Both men came under fire in the 1959 audit for their lax handling of county tax collections.

In 1960, the Internal Revenue Service charged that Brooks had filed a fraudulent federal income tax return for 1953. He claimed that he only earned $2,995 when he had actually earned $5,000 that year. Brooks had to post a $1,000 bond with the IRS, but he wasn't indicted.

"I'm not worried about it," Brooks told a *Constitution* reporter.

He won re-election as sheriff that year.

In addition to running some of his own liquor, Brooks also helped other county bootleggers avoid serious court actions in the county. One tactic he used was to refuse to locate bootlegging defendants who didn't show up for court and bring them in, telling the judge he "couldn't find" the defendants who had jumped bond.

At one point in 1963, Superior Court Judge Richard B. Russell III threatened to ask the governor for outside help if Brooks didn't bring in some missing bootlegging defendants. Russell also encouraged the county grand jury in February 1963 to look into local public officials who weren't doing their job, a clear shot at Brooks.

For his part, Brooks told that same grand jury and The *Atlanta Constitution* that his approach to illegal booze sales was to leave the enforcement up to state and federal officials, saying that too many law enforcement officials working on liquor cases would cause "confusion."

Brooks also told the *Constitution* in 1963, that he was doing the best he could on bootlegging and car thefts "in the country way we've been doing it for 20 years."

The Jackson Herald was openly critical of Brooks and his lack of willingness to enforce the law against bootlegging.

"It seems ridiculous that undercover revenue agents can come to Jackson County time after time and make purchases at dozens of establishments, yet local law enforcement agencies cannot find anyone to arrest for selling beer without a license," said an editorial in *The Jackson Herald* in June 1962.

Brooks also had other ways to help out local bootleggers. In one big case in 1962, authorities raided and got a padlock order in Jackson County Superior Court for an Amvets Club bootlegging operation south of Jefferson. The Amvets location was raided twice in early 1962.

But Brooks played what *The Jackson Herald* called "Legal Leap Frog." The sheriff pulled the Amvets case from Superior Court, where the padlock order was pending before Judge Russell, and gave it to the more amenable City Court Judge Early Stark. Padlock orders generally came from Superior Court and were a serious threat to bootleggers who were used to just paying a small bond then going right back to selling booze. Padlock orders would shut them down, perhaps forever.

On the Saturday morning after the Amvets raid, and just two days before the grand jury was to meet in February to consider indictments in Superior Court, City Court Judge Stark called the cases into his court. He was able to do that because at the time, the sheriff could put misdemeanor cases into either Superior Court or the City Court.

Stark fined the two men charged in the Amvets operation $350 each, and dismissed the rest of the charges. The club remained open, having avoided the threat of a Superior Court padlock order, thanks to the help of Sheriff Brooks and City Court Judge Stark.

"If this is the way our courts deal with illegal liquor offenders it is little wonder that bootlegging is a growing business in Jackson County," said an editorial in *The Jackson Herald* following the incident.

Brooks was clearly playing games with the case, in part to help himself. In 1961, Brooks had cut a deal with the county for his office to get part of the fines and forfeitures that came out of the City Court. That meant Brooks had a personal financial incentive to move misdemeanor bootlegging cases out of Superior Court and into City Court.

But that wasn't all of the problems. At the same time the Amvets Club was raided in 1962, officers also raided a bootlegging location run by two black brothers. That case was also put in Superior Court and there it stayed. Unlike the Amvets case, which was run by two white brothers, the black men's case didn't get special treatment by Brooks or the City Court.

That led to an editorial in *The Jackson Herald* decrying the move, saying "Equal justice seems absent..."

It isn't clear if that situation developed because of racism, or because the two black brothers hadn't paid the right people off.

Despite all of that, bootlegging wouldn't be Sheriff Brooks' eventual undoing. In 1963, Brooks and several associates were arrested on car theft charges out of Fulton County (Atlanta). Among the others indicted by a Fulton County grand jury were Brooks' son-in-law Donald Marlow; Brooks' partner in a used car business, Glenn Gee; George Boswell; and Albert Funderburk. (Marlow was later murdered in Pendergrass by two Gainesville brothers in a dispute over a woman; Funderburk would later reappear in court during the Hoard murder trials as having been an associate to bootlegger Park.)

Brooks was arrested by Jackson County Coroner Tom Conn since a coroner was the only person at that time with the authority to arrest a sheriff. Conn called the sheriff on a Friday afternoon and asked him to come to his Commerce office because he "had something to talk to him about."

Conn said when he called the sheriff, whom he had known for 18 years, he didn't tell him he had a warrant for his arrest. When Sheriff Brooks arrived in Commerce, Conn told him he was being put under arrest.

"For what?" Brooks asked.

Conn then read the warrant charging him with being an accessory-before-the-fact to an auto larceny.

"Then I told him I was turning him over to the GBI," Conn said. GBI agents were present when the warrant was read.

During the October 1963, trial in Fulton County, Mr. and Mrs. Richard Watkins testified that they stole cars in the Atlanta area at the direction of Sheriff Brooks. Watkins said he stole 30 or 40 autos with the aid of his wife and delivered them to the sheriff. Mrs. Watkins, age 19, told the jury that she helped her husband steal a late model Oldsmobile. She testified that she walked outside a church parking lot while her husband stole a car that met the sheriff's specifications. They were paid $100 for their services.

Brooks swore to the Fulton County Superior Court jury that he had never dealt in stolen cars. He denied that he had ever seen Watkins or his wife. But Brooks did admit during his trial that he had bought a tail section of a car from noted Commerce car thief Aubrey Joe Allen, brother of A. D. Allen. On the stand, Brooks admitted he knew Allen was an auto thief.

Also during the trial, Aubrey Joe Allen admitted Brooks had asked him to "talk" to Watkins, the key witness, before the trial. He declined to say what they discussed.

Brooks and Gee were convicted in October 1963, on the theft charges and sentenced to five years in prison. Brooks appealed to the Georgia Court of Appeals, which upheld the guilty verdict. (Brooks wasn't the only Georgia sheriff convicted in 1963. In neighboring Gwinnett County, Sheriff Dan Cole was convicted on illegal whiskey charges.)

Despite his conviction, Brooks continued to serve as sheriff for another year, until the end of his term.

In a parting shot on New Year's Eve 1964, just hours before he left office, Brooks released a North Carolina man from jail who had been charged with robbery. He released the prisoner to his deputy, Bartow Hall, without a required court hearing.

New Solicitor General Floyd Hoard was furious about the move.

"He didn't have any authority to let the man out on bond; there's no legal way it could have been done," Hoard said.

Just before Brooks was sent to Atlanta to serve his sentence in 1965, 259 people, many of whom were leaders in Jackson County, requested the courts suspend the sheriff's sentence. Brooks may have been a crooked sheriff, but he was liked by many in the county who didn't seem to care that he was a car thief.

5.
Car Thefts Rise As
Bootlegging Grows Stronger

Sheriff John B. Brooks had been convicted for car thefts in 1963 and that was a sign of just how big that illegal business had become in Jackson County in a very short time. Bootlegging and gambling had a long history in the county, but it was only in 1962 that stealing cars emerged as a large-scale enterprise.

It began with the theft of a 1961 Oldsmobile from the Jefferson Mills parking lot one Sunday morning in April 1962. That car was found off of Waterworks Road near Commerce, partially stripped. By the end of 1962, a front-page commentary in *The Jackson Herald* predicted that the illegal bootlegging in the county would be "pushed out" by the booming car theft rackets. That proved to be wrong, but the car theft operations did continue to grow in the coming years, especially in the area around the City of Commerce.

In early 1963, a slew of Jackson County car thefts made headlines: A dumping ground of car parts was discovered in some woods near Rogers Cemetery in Commerce; Commerce police found two stolen cars at the city's trash dump; a new 1963 Chevrolet was stolen from a Commerce auto dealer and found stripped; a stolen car was found near Banks-Jackson-Commerce Hospital in Commerce after thieves abandoned it when it ran out of gas; a stolen 1958 Chevrolet was found in the Brockton community near Jefferson by hunters who exchanged gunfire with the thieves; two cars were found in a barn on the Ed Kelly farm near Jefferson where they had cut one end out of the barn to drive the cars inside and used torches to cut them up; Commerce police had a wild chase through town early one Sunday morning with car thieves that ended when one of the cars rolled over; and state and federal authorities found three stolen cars in a Hoschton barn rented by a local bootlegger.

All of that was just in January.

And it wasn't just car thefts that were happening — a general lawlessness became pervasive around Commerce in early 1963. At one point, an explosion was set off in a bathroom of the Commerce Drive-In theater "causing pandemonium and the parking facilities of the theater were thrown into complete confusion by the reckless driving of vandals," said *The Commerce News*.

In February 1963, state and federal agents raided the A. D. Allen garage in Commerce where they found an assembly line for stripping cars and thousands of stolen auto parts scattered over three chicken houses. Former GBI Agent Ronnie Angel said each chicken house had its specific kinds of stripped parts.

"The first house had front end sections and doors; one of them was full of dashboards and bucket seats; and the other one full of tires, motors and transmissions," he said.

Across the road, behind Allen's home, state and federal law enforcement officers found over 150 stolen auto "hulls" that had been stripped for parts. Agents brought some 20 people from Atlanta who had their cars stolen to help identify the vehicles.

The case had begun after two youths were arrested in College Park. They admitted they had stolen over 250 cars and taken them to Allen's garage. The week after the raid, officers discovered some of the stolen auto parts being burned behind Allen's house. No court order to protect the evidence had been done.

Fulton County indicted 18 people from Jackson, Banks, Gwinnett and Madison counties related to the Allen raid in late February 1963. In May, Allen pled guilty at a Fulton County court hearing. News reports called the hearing a "great comedy" — some 14 other car theft defendants got the court to continue their cases for a variety of questionable reasons. After the hearing, Allen and the others were reported to have milled around in the courtroom "laughing" and joking with the various law enforcement officials.

"It was wild and wooly back then," recalled GBI agent Angel. "You couldn't drive down an old dirt road in Jackson County without finding a stolen car. It was all over — bad, bad."

One reason car thefts were so easy back then, Angel said, is that the state didn't have car titles.

"You could get the serial number ground off of it (a car) and they couldn't identify it and you were home free," he said.

The car thieves were also clever. Longtime Jefferson photographer Bob Freeman was once called by law enforcement to make a photo of a trac-tor-trailer that had been rigged as a mobile car-stripping setup. The rig had a hoist that could pull out the motor and a car could be completely disassembled inside the rig.

As time went on, the auto theft gangs became more ruthless. In neighboring Gwinnett County in 1964, three cops stumbled across a group of thieves stripping a stolen car. The cops were tied together and their bodies riddled with bullets.

In 1966, car thieves attempted to blow up a South Carolina auto parts dealer who had become a law enforcement informant. Two of those connected with that incident were originally from Jackson County.

While organized car thefts came to dominate much of the county's criminal news in the early 1960s, occasional raids on bootleggers continued. In December 1961, state agents raided a place just south of Jefferson that was an illegal bar and gambling joint and arrested two brothers.

In March 1962, authorities hit a house in South Jackson near Statham early one morning and confiscated 1,330 gallons of non-tax-paid liquor. The 229 cases of liquor were said to be the largest single bust in a decade.

In June 1962, 55 state agents raided five counties in Northeast Georgia, including Jackson. Among the places hit was a house across from the Elm Drive-In in Pendergrass where 300 cases of beer were confiscated and one man arrested. A few hours later, it was open for business again. It was raided again two weeks later, but it continued to reopen and operate.

That was a large raid, but the state's revenue commissioner was furious, saying that someone had "leaked" information about the raid to many of the bootleggers, who avoided getting caught.

In 1962, *Herald* reporters went to several of the bootlegging establishments and purchased beer, then reported on the purchases with directions to the establishments in a move to embarrass lax law enforcement officials.

In August 1963, a Jefferson policeman attempted to stop a suspicious truck driving through town. A chase ensued and the truck attempted to run the officer off the road. The officer then tried to shoot the tires out as the truck headed toward Gainesville.

Eventually, the truck stopped and the driver fled. Some 990 gallons of non-tax-paid whiskey were found in the truck and taken back to Jefferson where the booze was poured out by law enforcement officials on the town square as onlookers watched, an echo of a previous scene on the same square in 1918 when illegal moonshine had been poured out.

In April 1964, a large state raid hit Jackson, Barrow and Clarke counties. Some 63 men and women were arrested, 23 from Jackson. Much of the whiskey and beer found had South Carolina tax stamps, but not Georgia tax stamps.

Moonshining perhaps reached its zenith across the South in the early 1960s. That's despite the fact that the number of stills busted in 1963 was less than in 1955 across the nation — 18,460 in 1963 vs. 25,608 in 1955. But the size and production of the stills had changed, leading to a more commercial nature in the moonshine business.

A 1965 *Atlanta Constitution* article said that output from the nation's illegal moonshine stills had gone up by 44 million gallons per year despite there being fewer stills.

"Investigators say stills are getting bigger, more scientific and harder to find," the article stated.

That was evident in two large moonshine operations busted in Banks County in the rugged northern end of the Piedmont Circuit in 1965 and 1966.

In January 1965, federal and state agents raided one of North Georgia's largest moonshine operations ever found. About five miles west of the town of Homer, authorities found an operation that had a 30-foot conveyor running moonshine to a storage area from three large stills.

The capacity of the operation was one of the state's largest: 18,920 gallons of mash, 4,872 gallons of liquor, 2,200 pounds of malt, 1,335 empty jars and 13,200 lbs. of sugar. The operation was powered by a 25-horsepower boiler. The value of the moonshine alone was over $140,400. One man, Leverett Rylee, was arrested.

That same week, authorities also raided a still north of Homer where 11,500 gallons of mash was destroyed and one man was charged.

The second large operation was discovered in 1966 in a small house within

50 feet of I-85 near the Banks-Jackson County line. It was labeled by authorities as a "push-button still" that could produce 350 gallons of moonshine a day.

According to an *Atlanta Constitution* article about the raid, federal agents said 877 gallons of moonshine in plastic jugs were confiscated, along with 4,680 gallons of mash, 7,800 lbs. of sugar and five vehicles. Three people were arrested during the bust, including a teenage boy.

The increased capacity of moonshine operations is also seen in Georgia data from the early 1960s. In 1961, officials busted 3,390 stills, confiscated 77,600 gallons of moonshine and 2.28 million gallons of mash while 4,542 people were arrested. The number of stills hit went up to 3,701 in 1963, but fell down to 3,089 in 1964.

Despite that drop in the number of stills destroyed, more moonshine and mash was confiscated in 1964 than in 1961 — 89,200 gallons of moonshine and 4.8 million gallons of mash in 1964. Moonshining was no longer just the domain of rural mountain farmers; it had become industrialized, a big business involving millions of dollars.

One of the complicating aspects of Jackson County's bootlegging in the 1950s and 1960s was the small town of Arcade, three miles south of Jefferson. Arcade was the first town in an otherwise "dry" county to approve the sale of beer and wine in the 1940s.

By the 1950s, it had become a mecca for beer sales. The University of Georgia was nearby and thirsty students helped fuel the town's reputation for booze.

Much of Arcade's booze business was rooted in moonshining and bootlegging dating back long before the legal sale of beer. A 1972 *Atlanta Constitution* profile of Arcade quoted one longtime resident as saying the town legalized beer sales "because there was so much bootlegging going on we had to legalize it."

But there were controversies. In 1959, a group of citizens in Arcade attempted to have the town's charter revoked because there had been no functioning government in many years. That effort led to multiple elections and lawsuits and it wasn't until 1962 that the issue was resolved with the town keeping its charter.

During that three-year uproar, the state refused to issue beer and wine licenses to the town's stores because it lacked a government. When the town did reconstitute its government, it set the town's local beer and wine tax at only 10 cents a case, by far the lowest in the state.

The cheap beer drove sales even higher and the town became a major supplier of beer to bootleggers all over North Georgia. It wasn't unusual for a beer truck to park at one of the town's three legal retail stores and offload beer directly onto a bootlegger's truck to be hauled to another location. Some of those were to bootleggers in Jackson County, but many were to other nearby "dry" counties.

The town and its beer store owners deflected criticism of their questionable practices by using some of the income generated from the sales to make donations to various local groups, churches and schools. Jefferson native Gus Johnson remembers that when he was coaching part-time at Jefferson High School in the late 1960s, the first place he'd go for funds for new football uniforms was to the donation-generous beer stores in Arcade.

In the 1970s, state law was changed that no longer allowed Arcade to impose an artificially low tax. That, along with the growth of "wet" towns and counties, eventually caused Arcade's huge beer sales to dissipate.

On occasion in the 1960s, citizens spoke out in public about the bootlegging problems in the county. Local ministers sometimes railed on the radio against the illegal liquor business. *Jackson Herald* editor N. S. "Buddy" Hayden called for a crackdown on bootlegging as one of his New Year's resolutions in January 1962.

"It will be the duty of the Sheriff's department and all other law enforcement agencies to see to it that bootlegging is stopped in the county and that the word is passed 'through the channels' that this county will not tolerate vice and corruption," Hayden wrote.

In 1963, the grand jury ripped the sheriff's office under Sheriff Brooks for lax record-keeping:

"No records of cash bonds; laxity in handling court evidence; no sheriff's records of overall operations; that a prisoner operates the radio at the jail; no record of more than 500 highway violation cases made by the State Patrol in Jackson County..." said *The Jackson Herald* of the grand jury's report. The grand jury also called for larger court fines on bootleggers.

In 1965, a group of Pendergrass citizens connected with North Jackson Elementary School appeared before the grand jury to ask that a bootlegging joint near the school be declared a "public nuisance" and padlocked. The place was described as a "trailer with one room attached" located within 500 yards of the school.

Overall, however, that kind of citizen pushback was rare and muted by other citizens who didn't speak out, or who refused to convict those who had been charged. Most people knew what was going on with both the bootlegging and car thefts, but were scared. Fear ruled as people warned each other to stay quiet, or face getting "burned out."

After Hoard's death, former *Jackson Herald* editor Hayden recalled how he had gotten death threats in the early 1960s from Jackson County bootleggers:

"One caller told me to stand in front of the plate glass window of The Jackson Herald at 10 p.m. one evening and I would be shot. I stood there, a little frightened, but the shots never came."

Although the illegal operations in the area were sometimes deadly serious, there were also some humorous moments. Former GBI agent Angel recalled an incident in the early 1960s when he was working as a state trooper and chased a car from Banks County down to Commerce in Jackson County:

"He (the driver) ran into Dot's Drive-In — that was the hangout for all the car thieves, open 24 hours a day. I went wheeling into Dot's after he'd went in. I bailed out and went inside right behind him. There was a lot of people inside. I went in there, a big shot you know — I pulled up and adjusted my belt and everything— and said, 'I don't know who you are, but you're going to have to leave sooner or later and when you leave, I'll be waiting on you.' I turned around and went back outside — all four tires on my car had been cut. I took my tail and went bloop, bloop, bloop down the road."

6.
Floyd "Fuzzy" Hoard

It was into this cauldron of public corruption and widespread illegal activity that Floyd "Fuzzy" Hoard arrived in Jackson County. Hoard was born in 1927 in Fayette County, just south of Atlanta, the fifth of nine children. How he got the nickname "Fuzzy" as a child isn't clear, according to his family.

Growing up during the Depression, most of the Hoard children left school at age 16 to find work in the local textile mills. But Floyd remained in school and graduated first in his high school class of 1944. A football star at Spalding County High School, he turned down 15 other scholarship offers in order to attend the University of Georgia. Hoard, a hard-hitting offensive lineman, was named co-captain of the freshman team.

But the young Hoard left UGA after two quarters to enlist in the U.S. Navy. Following a 17-month stint in the military, he accepted a football scholarship to Georgia Military College in Milledgeville, where he was named "All Southeastern Guard."

After receiving a liberal arts degree from GMC in 1948, he taught at the school for three years while attending night classes at Mercer University. Hoard also played baseball at Mercer and for three years — 1950-1953 — for a minor league summer baseball team, the Eastman Dodgers of the Georgia State League. He had a batting average of .380 over the three years.

In 1950, Hoard married a Jefferson girl, Imogene Westmoreland, and two years later, finished his degree work at Mercer University. For a while he taught school and coached.

When Hoard's father-in-law, George Westmoreland, suffered a stroke in

1952, the Hoards moved to Jefferson. Floyd soon enrolled in the LaSalle University extension program and began studying for the Georgia Bar exam. For a time during his studies, he ran a small Dairy Kreme snack shack on the Winder Road in Jefferson.

Within two and a half years, he had finished his law studies and passed the bar exam. He began his law practice in Jefferson in 1955 with his father-in-law on the second floor of the brick Westmoreland Building across from the county courthouse.

George Westmoreland wasn't just any lawyer. He had held several public offices during his long career, including solicitor of the City Court in the 1920s and had served as mayor of Jefferson. At the time of his stroke in 1952, Westmoreland was serving another term as City Court solicitor, having been appointed by the governor in 1950 to fill an unexpired vacancy. Westmoreland had a lot of connections and that opened doors for son-in-law Hoard.

Attorney James Horace Wood later described Hoard's relationship with Westmoreland this way:

"He was a rarity among lawyers. He'd learned most of his law at the elbow of his father-in-law, George W. Westmoreland, one of the most distinguished lawyers in Jackson County. Combined with his own home-study courses, this had enabled him to pass the Bar examination without formal law-school training."

Hoard gained early prominence in the legal profession when he and attorney Wood were appointed to defend James Fulton Foster, who was accused of the murder of Jefferson merchant Charlie Drake in 1956. It was Hoard's first murder case.

Drake was shot and killed in June 1956 when an intruder broke into his home in the early evening as Drake was watching television. Drake was known to carry around several thousand dollars in cash, which was apparently the motive for the break-in. The intruder surprised Drake and the elderly man ran for his bedroom to get a gun. He got off one shot before the intruder shot back and killed him. Drake's wife was beaten and knocked unconscious while trying to telephone for help.

Hoard was one of the first people on the scene of the murder and helped put Drake's body on the stretcher. Foster, a house-painter from Greer, S. C., was charged in the slaying after having been picked up on unrelated charges. Foster, who was renting a room in nearby Gainesville at the time, had been in

Jackson County the night of the murder with several companions looking for bootleg beer in the town of Pendergrass. But Foster hadn't been in Jefferson and didn't murder Drake.

Despite having several witnesses who put him at other locations during the time of the shooting, Foster was convicted for the murder based on the testimony of Mrs. Drake, who said in court that Foster was the intruder. He was sentenced to death in the electric chair.

Wood and Hoard worked on an appeal until the actual killer, "Rocky" Rothschild, who was in a South Carolina jail on other charges, made a dramatic confession to the Drake murder in 1958. Foster was only days away from being put to death when Rothschild confessed. The case made national headlines.

In a famous scene played out in front of the Jackson County courthouse on July 8, 1958, Foster and Rothschild met face-to-face, along with lawyers Hoard and Wood and hundreds of onlookers and photographers. Foster's wife embraced Rothschild during the meeting and thanked him for sparing her husband by confessing. The moment overtook her and she fainted. Hoard picked her up and carried her to the front porch of the old county jail nearby.

The Foster-Rothschild case made Hoard, Wood and Foster celebrities. After Foster's release from jail in 1958, Hoard and his family, Foster and his family (he had seven children), and Wood took a vacation together to Florida. (Wood later wrote a book about the case, *Nothing But The Truth.* In his book, Wood said that he and Hoard clashed during the case, especially after Hoard took the position before the Rothschild confession that Foster should take a plea deal to avoid the death penalty.)

That case gave Hoard a high profile, but it also brought him into contact with a notorious Jackson County criminal, A. D. Allen of Commerce. Allen was a local bootlegger, but also ran other criminal enterprises, including car theft. On the night of Drake's murder, Allen was said to have been the getaway driver for Rothschild. He was convicted as an accomplice in the murder in 1958, but that conviction was eventually overturned by the Georgia Supreme Court.

After Hoard's murder, Allen would become a prime suspect because of his extensive underworld dealings in liquor, stolen cars and other illegal activities in the area.

Hoard reportedly loved the law. N. S. "Buddy" Hayden, who had been editor of *The Jackson Herald* in the early 1960s, later recalled in a column in the *Athens Banner-Herald* a comment Hoard had made to him about the legal profession.

"Law is the most perfect profession," Hoard told Hayden. "You can do so much to help. You can be such a good force. You can aid those who need aid and you can prosecute those who you know are guilty."

Hoard's passion for justice and his flair for words can be seen in two letters to the editor he penned in the late 1950s. In July 1958, Hoard wrote a letter to *The Jackson Herald* calling on citizens to be better informed "as to what is going on in public business." It's not clear exactly what he was referring to, but Hoard said the public should appreciate those who "bring to the attention of the public irregularities in public affairs. Such irregularities breed power politics; power politics breeds dictatorship and destroys democracy," he said.

In 1959, the bombshell Jackson County audit had uncovered a number of serious problems, including the fact that at least one local company had not been paying property taxes for many years. Auditors found that the county's board of tax equalizers had not assessed the property because the owner had made "large donations for public welfare."

That was illegal — tax assessors weren't supposed to consider a company's donations as an offset for paying property taxes.

In a letter to the editor about that issue, Hoard challenged *Herald* editor Tom Williams to dig into the matter.

"Fire your guns from the hips, Mr. Editor, and stand unyielding against all counterattacks."

Hoard went on to blast the companies that had not paid their taxes:

"Why do these companies give to welfare and what welfare are they giving to? Are they giving to welfare because they love Jackson County? No, if they loved Jackson County they would be paying Jackson County taxes on their property... Can it be that the companies are promoting their own control over whatever they contribute to?"

Without naming names, Hoard then took a personal shot at a prominent local civic leader who hadn't paid his taxes:

"Could it be, Mr. Editor, that one of our most outstanding citizens was trying to beat Jackson County out of taxes which he rightfully owed and

that his armor of virtue got to shining so brightly that he was forced to return them for taxes, less someone discover his failures and cast a pall of gloom over his shining coat of arms."

Hoard said some of the county's leadership wanted to "whitewash" the wrongdoings uncovered by the audit and he called on editor Williams to "sound the clarion call" about the issue:

"The truth shall always conquer evil to make us free. The process may be slow, but in this country the truth will win."

Hoard was the county government attorney during the 1959 audit scandal, having succeeded his father-in-law in the position in 1956. When auditors presented the scathing results to the three-man Jackson County Board of Commissioners in late May 1959, the group quickly adjourned the meeting (two of the three board members had been implicated in the audit for questionable county financial deals.)

After the commissioners bolted the meeting at the courthouse, Hoard directed the auditors to stay around and hand out copies of the document to the press. Hoard wanted the public to know how deep problems ran in county government.

For a short time in late 1959 and early 1960, Hoard served as managing editor of *The Jackson Herald* for newspaper owner, John Holder. Editor Williams had left *The Herald* in October 1959 for the newspaper in Oconee County. Holder had become too feeble to run the newspaper, so Hoard, who was Holder's attorney, stepped in for a few months as editor.

There were several editorials in that time that Hoard wrote dealing with the county's bootlegging problem and general corruption. Hoard wrote one editorial in October 1959 after solicitor general Alfred Quillian and Sheriff John B. Brooks paid back the $9,000 for the insolvent bonds they had sold the county. Hoard said the payback was a "baby step" in correcting the wrongs that had been uncovered in the 1959 county audit and he called on the public to be more aware of the corruption around them:

"It is possible to endure a thing for so long that it becomes a part of our way of life. It is possible to evade responsibility for so long that it too becomes a part of our way of life."

Another editorial was written in December 1959, following the defeat of a referendum to legalize the sale of beer in Jefferson. That editorial laments the Jefferson vote, saying:

"Are we hopelessly lost; must we yield always, or is there some way somehow to rid our county of the yoke of fear and tyranny which enchains us. Must we forever remain silent and enduring to the evils of bootleg beer and whiskey." (Hoard had also written a newspaper editorial before the vote endorsing it.)

During his brief stint as editor, Hoard also began a fiction series in *The Herald* entitled, "It Couldn't Happen Here." The project was supposed to have six parts, but only two were published before the newspaper was sold by Holder and another editor was brought in by the new owners.

In those first two parts of his fiction story, Hoard spoke of a small, Southern town (Jefferson thinly disguised) that had been corrupted by local organized crime.

"This series is intended to make us all do a little thinking about the welfare of our county," Hoard wrote in his introduction.

In the story, "John Doe" is found one Sunday morning murdered and strapped to the Confederate monument on the town square. The man apparently behind the murder was kingpin "Cheater Swindle" who had been "earmarked by the federal government as the king of the racketeers."

A line in the story by a third character (who was apparently Hoard's alter-ego) echoed a sentiment that Hoard would repeat again and again about how good citizens were complicit in the rackets:

"When a criminal organization is conceived in evil, born by an unsuspecting society, married to the respectability, then honest citizens have an impossible situation... (he) wondered if he and other law-abiding citizens would ever really take the stand to restore law and order to the community."

Those who knew him say Hoard's personality was affable. Jimmy Booth, who was editor of *The Jackson Herald* in 1964 when Hoard was elected solicitor general, said that Hoard had a "terrific personality." Booth said that Hoard would sometimes drop into the newspaper office to chat with the people there. Because he'd once managed the paper, Hoard felt very at home in the office, he said.

"He made friends very easily," Booth said of Hoard.

Hoard also had a droll sense of humor that sometimes came through in his comments to the press. Shortly after taking office as solicitor general in December 1964, Hoard began raiding area bootlegging joints. He told the *Atlanta Constitution*, "This is just the beginning... as soon as I learn to catch car thieves, we're going to start doing that."

Former GBI agent Ronnie Angel, who worked closely with Hoard to catch bootleggers and later coordinated the investigation into his murder, said Hoard could be fun-loving, but was serious about his work.

"Around me, he was jovial," Angel recalled. "We would cut up and joke with each other. When it came to the job, he was very serious. From my perspective, he was very dedicated to do what he said he would do and clean up the bootlegging."

In his book about the famous Drake murder case of 1956, attorney Wood described Hoard this way: "Hoard was a short, roundish man, 29 years old. Unsmiling and serious-minded, he seemed devoted to his profession."

Former *Jackson Herald* editor Helen Buffington knew Hoard from their church association and she also covered his murder and the following trials.

"He was an easy-going sort with a rather soft voice," she said. "He wasn't one who did a lot of talking, but you knew that when he did talk, it was worth listening to."

Hoard's youngest daughter, Vivian, recalled her father's athletic ability.

"He could do a flip in the air without touching the ground with his hands," she said. Hoard's wife said he could easily walk on his hands, too. And he loved to hit baseballs to son "Dickey" in the large field in front of their rural home.

Hoard also coached a local women's softball team for several years, recalled Jacque Wilkes.

"He was a good coach, not mean or anything," she said.

Ever the athlete, Hoard continued to play baseball and softball in local mill and town leagues up until the time of his death. One of those who played ball with Hoard was Cecil Buffington, now Jefferson's unofficial historian.

"I played on the Lions Club softball team my junior and senior year (of high school) with him," Buffington recalled. "Hoard played first base. He was a left-handed power-hitter that would bat from the left side and hit home runs over the track. I don't think anybody in the league hit the ball farther than Hoard."

Buffington said Hoard was just a regular guy.

"He was just a normal guy out to have fun playing softball with his friends."

In addition to his position as county attorney and a brief stint as newspaper editor, Hoard was also feeling the call to jump into the county's politics. In 1960, he ran for City Court Judge against incumbent Early Stark, whose leniency on bootlegging cases was well-known. But Hoard lost that election to Stark by 700 votes. The county wasn't yet ready to change the status quo.

Hoard wasn't alone in his pursuit to right some of the wrongs in Jackson County. His wife, Imogene, was a strong supporter of his convictions and was tough in her own right.

In October 1960, Jefferson's town doctor found that out the hard way. The doctor and his wife had split and she was boarding with a landlady in town. One Tuesday morning, the doctor went to the boarding house, banging on the door, cursing and trying to get inside to see his estranged wife. The landlady came to the door with a gun and told him to leave.

That afternoon, the doctor's estranged wife was visiting Imogene Hoard when the doctor showed up in the Hoard's front yard. When Imogene saw him, she got a .32 pistol and fired a shot to the left of his car, according to an *Atlanta Constitution* article.

"If you get out of the car, I'll kill you," she told the doctor.

He left, but later took out a warrant for Imogene. She was arrested by her own brother, Jefferson Police Chief Albert Westmoreland, and released on bond. The case was apparently later dropped.

The doctor was later arrested for disorderly conduct in Jefferson and indicted in South Georgia on kidnapping charges related to his family disputes.

While the bootlegging, corruption and car thefts had gotten a lot of headlines in the 1950s and 1960s as Hoard settled into his legal career, the Jefferson and Jackson County community was changing in a different way as well. The post-WWII economic boom had begun to turn around the county's decline in population. Factory jobs, especially in textile manufacturing, were luring people off the farm, a movement that had a huge cultural impact in small towns all around the South.

The City of Jefferson was no different. After the end of WWII, the Bryan family, which owned Jefferson Mills, expanded the mill's operations and undertook a large number of community civic improvement projects. Among other things, they began a mill newspaper; built the football stadium for Jefferson's first high school football team in 1947; fixed the town's swimming pool; and began an annual kids' day camp program in the summer.

Perhaps the mill's biggest impact, however, was to put money and leadership into the city's school system. Jefferson had a long history of quality education. The University of Georgia was nearby and that had made access to college easy for local students. In addition, the town's Martin Institute was a well-known boarding school that had a long list of distinguished alumni. The Martin Institute facility burned in 1942, but by that time it was part of the Jefferson City School System. After WWII, Jefferson Mills poured thousands of dollars into the school system, a practice it would continue until it was sold by the Bryan family in the 1980s.

The community was changing in other ways as well in the 1950s and 1960s. In 1965, Interstate I-85 opened in the county, creating a link to Atlanta and up to the Northeast that would bring major changes to the community. Other manufacturing plants began locating in the county in the mid-1960s and the chamber of commerce was growing. And despite the turmoil of the era over school desegregation, the move toward integrating Jackson County schools was peaceful.

Cecil Buffington, who was a local high school student in the early 1960s, said the atmosphere of the era was "laid back."

"I think the atmosphere could be described as casual and laid back in the 1950's and 1960's in Jefferson," he said. "It seemed like no one ever got in too much of a hurry."

For decades, there had been a local joke about Jefferson's lack of progress: It was in Jefferson in 1842 that Crawford W. Long performed the first surgery using anesthesia. The joke was that Long had put Jefferson to sleep and it had never awoken. But by the mid-1960s, Jefferson was starting to wake up. There was a sense of optimism as Jackson County moved away from a "cotton-and-corn" economy to manufacturing.

So although there was an underworld of lawlessness and public corruption in the community, there was also growth and progress. The two worlds — one of crime, the other of prosperity — co-existed. And to a large extent, the county's good citizens, along with many of its business and civic leaders, turned a blind eye to the crime and corruption. Even when local citizens did acknowledge the lawlessness, it was often with a distorted view.

That was reflected in a newspaper editorial in *The Jackson Herald* in 1963 which called on local citizens to take a more active role in prosecuting local thugs.

"We, the supposedly 'responsible citizens,' through our actions or lack of action have actually encouraged the emergence of such a state of affairs."

True enough, but then the editorial veers off and blames the lack of respect for the law on the 1954 Brown vs. Board of Education school integration controversy, saying that court ruling had "nurtured disrespect for law." In other words, the community's corruption problems were somebody else's fault.

In the same vein of denial, a prominent Jefferson merchant was quoted by the *Atlanta Constitution* after Hoard's murder as saying, "The Floyd Hoard murder just don't register the type of people who live here."

Indeed, most people in the community were "responsible citizens." Many had no direct contact with the illegal booze or car theft businesses.

Still, there was a conspiracy of silence among the decent citizens in Jackson County about its criminal underworld and its corrupt public officials, a silence driven by fear and a large measure of denial. As a result, the local bootleggers and car thieves were becoming stronger and bolder.

As someone deeply enmeshed in the local judicial system, Floyd Hoard saw the community's silence more clearly than many others. That was evident in a February 1963 editorial Hoard wrote for *The Jackson Herald*. Although he was no longer editor, Hoard occasionally penned articles for the newspaper.

Writing in response to the recent bust of the A. D. Allen car theft operation in Commerce, Hoard put the blame for organized crime squarely on local citizens:

"In this matter, ultimately the blame can fall on no other shoulders than those of our citizens. Many of us are like an ostrich; we like to do our undercover work in order to avoid seeing what is going on at the surface. Let's stop burying our heads in the sand!"

7.

The "Old Man"

Andrew Clifford Park was born in Pendergrass on August 17, 1891, the son of Junius and Eula Gilbert Park. He was apparently named for an uncle, also "Andrew Clifford Park" and perhaps his grandfather, Andrew M. Park.

His parents divorced when he was young and Park grew up with his mother, a school teacher, in the home of his maternal grandmother, Sarah Gilbert. Both of Park's parents remarried, his mother moving to Gillsville and eventually to Atlanta where she died in 1959. His father was a bartender who worked in towns around the Southeast. He died in Greenville, S.C., in 1947. Despite having a school teacher mom, Park only went through the 8th grade.

"He was a smart man, but not an educated one," said his daughter Diane.

Park had an older brother, Harry. According to Diane, the brothers were very close.

"They were typical boys who enjoyed playing outside, roughhousing, fishing, and aggravating each other," she said Park's mother had told her.

When Park's mother remarried and moved to Atlanta, Harry went with her. But Cliff stayed in Pendergrass and lived with a "spinster aunt in the house in which he was born," Diane said.

Just after his 27th birthday in 1918, Park was drafted into the military. He was single at the time, of medium build with blue eyes, according to his military records. He listed his occupation as "farmer" and that he was self-employed. Park, along with 21 other men from Jackson County, was sent to Camp Greenleaf in Northwest Georgia on the grounds of Chickamauga National Battlefield

Park. It was a training camp for medical officers being sent to Europe during WWI.

Park served overseas from September 1918 to March 1919 as a private in a medical unit. He was there only two months before the war ended on Nov. 11, 1918. According to Diane, Park didn't talk about his military service. He reportedly got a severe case of pneumonia while serving and was hospitalized for a short time while in the army.

On returning to the states in the spring of 1919, Park resumed living in Pendergrass with his aunt. In 1921 at age 29, he married 19-year-old Mae Lou Hartly. The two had met at a camp meeting and "were smitten with each other right away," said Diane.

"They were completely devoted to each other and were married for 57 years."

The two settled into the house where Park was born.

Park mostly kept a low profile in the community. His name is seldom mentioned in the local social columns that were popular in the newspaper at the time. In 1930, he was mentioned twice, once when a step-sister came to visit him and once when a church group met in one of his pastures for a social event.

In 1940, Park was listed in a newspaper article as one of around 30 Jackson County farmers who had more than a bale per acre from cotton production the previous year. He was listed has having had 557 lbs. per acre for 4.3 acres of cotton.

At some point during the Depression, Park and Mae Lou ran a general store in the small town.

"I remember them talking about rationing, coupons, and hard times," said Diane. "Like many people during that time, they raised chickens, milked cows, churned butter, made soap, butchered hogs, sewed clothes from chicken feed sacks, and grew many of their own vegetables. Clifford really didn't talk about it much, but Mae Lou said people just learned to do without."

In the 1940s, the Parks adopted Diane, who was actually their great-niece.

"Mae Lou and my grandmother were sisters," recalled Diane. "After my parents divorced, Clifford and Mae Lou legally adopted me. Since I was six years old and already knew and loved my birth parents, they never asked me to call them mother and daddy. They allowed me to see and visit them whenever it was possible."

Diane said Cliff was a doting, but sometimes overprotective dad.

"Clifford definitely doted on me, so I guess I was somewhat spoiled. However, he and Mae Lou were strict and overprotective. Although I didn't appreciate it at the time, I realize now that because they were the age of my friend's grandparents and much older than most parents, they were scared and just concerned about my safety and well-being."

Diane said Cliff was a quiet man at home.

"He was a very quiet man and very reserved. There was not one time in my childhood that I recall him ever raising his voice to me. When I practiced the piano, marimba, or clarinet, he would come into the room, sit quietly, and listen. Whether I deserved it or not, he would always say 'that was mighty pretty, Diane.' I relished hearing those words."

Cliff wasn't a fan of movies, Diane recalled. He watched the news and baseball on television and was a huge Yankees fan.

"I grew up hearing all about the Mighty Five — Ruth, Mantle, Gehrig, DiMaggio, and Berra," she said.

Both Cliff and Mae Lou enjoyed gardening.

"That was their hobby," Diane said. "Before it became too physically demanding and time-consuming, they both liked having a big garden. After the vegetables were harvested, Clifford would sack them up and take them to friends and neighbors. For as long as he was able, he loved doing that."

Diane said Clifford was a "gentleman." He usually wore a tie and suspenders and outside, he wore a stylish fedora hat.

"To me, he was the epitome of a Southern Gentleman," she said. "He always tipped his hat to a lady and stood when a woman entered the room."

That sentiment was also expressed by one of the law enforcement officials who helped convict Park for Hoard's murder.

"He was very quiet, very reserved, old country gentleman," said former GBI agent Ronnie Angel about Park's demeanor. "He was very cordial."

Park was known as a "leading citizen" in the community, according to a mention of his name in an obituary when an uncle died. But in 1959, when he ran for a seat on the Pendergrass City Council, he got the second-lowest number of votes, coming in seventh out of eight candidates.

It's not clear when Park got into moonshining and bootlegging, but his name appears on a federal court listing of cases in October 1917. He was charged with removal and concealment of liquor.

A look at court records by the *Athens Banner-Herald* following Hoard's murder found that Park had run-ins with Jackson County law enforcement in 1925 when he pled guilty to carrying a concealed pistol. In 1928 and again in 1942, Park was charged with selling liquor. In the 1942 case, Park was found not guilty while five other bootleggers were found guilty during the same court hearing.

According to a *Gainesville Times* story, Park was convicted in federal court for bootlegging in 1946 and drew a $2,000 fine and five years of probation.

There is a federal case from 1922 of an A. C. Parks for violating the Prohibition Act, but his home location listed is Lumpkin County, Ga. The charges include possession of a 60-gallon still, 33 fermenters, 9,000 gallons of beer, 6 bushels of meal, 4 bushels of malt, 400 lbs. of sugar, 4 barrels, 6 kegs all used to make liquor. Also confiscated was 60 gallons of whiskey, 60 gallons of brandy and 60 gallons of rum.

It could be that Park was caught in Lumpkin County making moonshine and the arresting agents simply listed his home at that location. There are no other A. C. Park(s) shown in the Lumpkin County area around that time. In any event, after multiple delays, he was found not guilty on the charges in federal court in 1925.

In August 1958, Park, along with 54 others, was rounded up in a massive North Georgia raid designed to cripple the flow of illegal liquor into the Atlanta market. Park was listed by authorities as being a "kingpin" in the illegal liquor trade. Authorities believed they had an "air tight" case against Park, but he managed to escape punishment in federal court.

In 1959, the Jackson County Grand Jury indicted Park on two counts of liquor violations. A newspaper story on that indictment said Park was again referred to by federal agents as the "kingpin of Northeast Georgia bootleggers." That 1959 case was apparently never called to trial.

In 1960, Park and two other local men were convicted on federal charges for selling moonshine. Park's original sentence was for four years in prison and a $4,000 fine. Park appealed and in 1962, served one year in federal prison in Atlanta. He didn't personally sell moonshine anymore after that, leaving that part of his business to associates.

Park's only local county court bootlegging conviction on record was after Hoard raided his operation in 1967.

Daughter Diane said Park never discussed his legal issues around her or with her. She didn't know in advance that he was headed to federal prison in 1962.

"When I arrived home from Jefferson High School one day, Clifford wasn't home," she recalled. "When I asked Mae Lou where he was, she tearfully told me he had been taken to the Federal Penitentiary in Atlanta where he would serve time for one year. I had no idea that he wouldn't be there when I got home. Mae Lou said he didn't tell me because he didn't want to upset, worry, or ruin my school day. He was like that when it came to me."

The Associated Press sent two top reporters to the community after Hoard's murder and they interviewed a number of people. Ironically, one of the people they spoke with was Park. Park admitted to the *AP* that he had "run a little whiskey."

For a time in the early 1960s, Park had gotten his beer from Arcade where it was legally sold, but at some point Arcade was "cut off" as his supplier. The reason for that isn't clear. Former bootlegger Troy Lee Griffith said that Park and the leading beer and wine store owners in Arcade had a falling out in the 1960s.

Whatever the reason, after being cut off from buying his beer and wine in Arcade, Park began buying beer from the Negro American Legion Club in Commerce, which had a federal license to buy beer. (It would later come out that Jackson County Sheriff L. G. "Snuffy" Perry had arranged that deal for Park.) An employee of Park's bootlegging operation would use a 1.5-ton truck to haul about 200 cases at a time from Commerce to Pendergrass, where it would be resold at one of Park's establishments. The Legion would make about 25 cents per case.

Park's Pendergrass bootlegging operation at his house was wide open. That was the way it had long been, according to Gus Johnson. Johnson was a student at Jefferson High School in the early 1950s and remembered how Park operated at his Pendergrass house.

"We'd load up the car and pull up at Mr. Cliff's place and they'd come to the door and ask, 'How old are you?' Not that it mattered, you know. You'd place your order and pull up. There was a little barn out back and they'd bring what you ordered out from the barn. It was just like a little drive-thru service at McDonald's now."

By the 1960s, Park's operation had grown. No secret passwords were necessary to enter the bootlegging garage at Park's house, which was on Hwy. 129 in Pendergrass in full view of passersby.

GBI agent Angel testified in court in 1968 that "this was an open operation and there was nothing hidden about the thing." It was a "supermarket" operation. Park's bootlegging garage was filled with large coolers, neon signs and had chips, boiled eggs and pickles for sale, too. It had a television for Park to watch when he wasn't selling booze. Beer sold for $2-$3 a six pack; vodka and gin, $4 a pint; and liquor $5 a pint.

Park worked the operation at the garage next to his house, but other people ran locations around the county that Park controlled. At Park's "yellow house" operation, customers didn't go inside. They walked up to the front door, which had a hole cut in the upper part with a shelf that folded down. Customers would place their order and the booze would be handed through the hole in the door to them.

One of Park's bootlegging employees at the "yellow house" said that location took in anywhere from $300 to $1,400 a week. He turned all the money over to Park twice a day, morning and evening. The employee was paid $100 a week regardless of how much he sold, he later said.

GBI agent Angel remembers that Park's enterprise at his house was so busy, people would jokingly complain that the sheriff's department should send deputies to "direct traffic" for customers.

On one of his undercover buys, Angel said he asked Park if he'd been busy that day.

"I've been so busy that I haven't been able to watch the ballgame," Park replied.

Somewhere along the way, Park came to dominate the area's bootlegging business and was labeled a "kingpin" by state law enforcement officials. But it doesn't appear as if Park was feared on a personal level the way A. D. Allen and his car theft gang had been.

There was a widely-circulated legend that Park once had a dispute with a black tenant farmer and threw the woman's baby into a fire. And there was a widespread fear by citizens that if they talked about the bootleggers, they would be "burned out."

That "burning out" theme was hinted at by *Jackson Herald* editor Tom Williams in the late 1950s. Williams said that he had received numerous threats over the years of his crusading against bootleggers. During one period when "hoodlums were burning out their opposition," Williams said he was advised to get a gun for personal protection. He got a gun and a "toter's permit" to carry it. One night, he heard a noise around his house, got his gun and went to investigate.

"The armed editor was slow on the draw since the automatic got caught in his pocket and 'damn near shot his leg off getting it out," Williams wrote in

1959. "The gun has rested in the safe ever since."

There may have been some "burning outs" as Williams suggested, but violence against rivals in the liquor business didn't appear to be Park's main way of gaining the upper hand. More likely, Park paid for protection and perhaps had local law enforcement officials help him keep rivals in line.

That idea is reinforced in a 2013 letter former Barrow County hit-man Billy Sunday Birt sent to his son, Billy Stonewall Birt. The letter is included in Stonewall's 2017 book, *"Rock Solid, In His Own Words"* about his father's life of crime. In the letter, Billy Sunday Birt had this to say about Park:

"Back then boot-leg whiskey was a big money maker. A. C. Cliff Park was the kingpin when it came to buying and selling alcohol in Jackson County. Anyone who dealt in making or selling whiskey, beer or wine in his area, A. C. got a percentage of it or he would have them shut down. Him and A. D. (Allen) got along with each other because they were mostly in separate businesses."

Park was certainly involved in the county's politics. In his interview with the *Associated Press* after Hoard's murder, but before he was charged in the case, Park admitted he contributed to local political campaigns.

"I helped him when he ran and he knows it," Park told the *AP* about one unnamed local candidate. "He and his wife came over here. They asked me to vote for him, and I did."

Park having protection was especially true for the years that John B. Brooks was sheriff. Brooks and Park were neighbors and both were in the liquor business.

"Him (Park) and John B. ran the county back in them days," said former bootlegger Troy Lee Griffith.

Park kept a low profile overall, according to Griffith.

"I made liquor for old man Cliff," he said. "What he done, he made it... he was just the money man. He kept a low profile."

It could be that Park became the local bootlegging "kingpin" simply because he had done it so long and outlived everyone else in the business. He was known in the bootlegging business as "the Old Man."

Park was himself once the victim of some of his moonshining associates. On a Saturday night in early January 1946, a man knocked on the front door of Park's home in Pendergrass. Mae Lou went to see who it was. A man shoved her through the house to the back porch while a second man went to the bedroom where Cliff was trying to get a gun from his bureau drawer. The second intruder grabbed the gun from Park and forced him onto the back porch with Mae Lou.

At gunpoint, the two were then herded into a bathroom where they were robbed of their wallets. As a gunman stood watch, other members of the robbery gang rolled Park's safe out of the house and loaded it onto a truck. The group then fled the scene, warning Park to remain quiet as they left. They had cut the house's telephone line, so the Parks had to walk to a neighbor's house to call for help.

Park initially said the safe contained $10,000 in cash and $12,500 in war bonds and some personal papers. A couple of weeks later, two men with ties to Dawson County's moonshine community, Jack Cantrell and Clint Chastain, were arrested and charged with the robbery.

Cantrell, 19, was one of the early moonshine "runners" who raced at Lakewood Park in Atlanta in the formative years of NASCAR. Before the Parks' robbery, Cantrell had been convicted for manslaughter for having run over an 18-year-old girl on a sidewalk along Ponce de Leon Avenue in Atlanta in 1945. He was out of jail on appeal when the Park robbery happened.

But Cantrell didn't stand trial for the robbery. He was gunned down in Atlanta in May 1946 by a man he owed $450 in a bootlegging debt. About the same time, a third man, Reggie Crawford, age 17, was arrested and charged in the Park robbery.

It turned out that the Park robbery was one of a rash of safe robberies across the state in 1946 done by a loose-knit gang of moonshiners led by famous race car driver and moonshiner Roy Hall of Dawson County. Cantrell and Crawford had been a part of that group.

Hall was convicted in Jackson County in the fall of 1946 for robbing Park of $50,000 ($645,000 in 2018 dollars) and sentenced to 2-10 years in prison. It isn't clear what other members of the group besides Hall were directly involved in the robbery — Hall was apparently the only one convicted.

8.

Hoard Becomes A Lawman

Although he had failed to oust City Court Judge Early Stark in the 1960 election, Floyd Hoard decided to try the political arena again. By the mid-1960s, he had become firmly entrenched in the county's legal and political system. The 1956-58 Foster-Rothschild case made him a rising star. His role as county attorney in pushing to clean up the mess found in the 1959 Jackson County government audit burnished his reputation for being straightforward.

By 1962, he was trusted as an honest member of the local bar, as seen in the wake of the Clinkscales scandal. Following Judge Maylon Clinkscales' disbarment, his attorney sued him for not having paid his legal bills and alleged that Clinkscales was transferring assets out of his own name to avoid payment. Judge Richard Russell III froze Clinkscales' assets in early 1962 and appointed Hoard as "temporary receiver" to take charge of those assets until the lawsuit could be settled.

In 1964, Hoard decided to jump into the political arena again by running for Solicitor General (now district attorney) of the Piedmont Judicial Circuit, which includes Jackson, Barrow and Banks counties. The circuit was created in 1923, a few years after Barrow County was created from part of Jackson County.

Former *Jackson Herald* editor Jimmy Booth wrote a column about one of Hoard's stories from the 1964 race. A few nights before the vote and after a long day of campaigning, Hoard went to bed early, before his wife, Imogene. When she later came to retire for the night, she found him sleeping crosswise in the bed.

"Floyd, you've got to get on one side or the other," she told him.

"Which side's got the most votes?" he quipped.

Booth recalled that overall, the 1964 election was fairly quiet.

"People just voted and didn't say too much publicly," he said.

Hoard ran for the solicitor general's seat in 1964 on a "clean-up" the circuit campaign in tandem with former state Senator Mark Dunahoo of Barrow County, who was challenging Russell for Judge of Superior Court. Hoard's wife Imogene recalled that Floyd "couldn't stand" how open the bootlegging operations had become.

After the votes were counted, Hoard had ousted the incumbent solicitor general Alfred Quillian of Barrow County, by taking both Banks and Jackson counties in the September elections. Quillian won his home county of Barrow, but not by enough to overcome Hoard's lead. Hoard won by a total of 374 votes.

Defeating Quillian was a big deal. The Winder native was from a long line of leading lawyers and judges in the state and had served as solicitor general since 1957. Quillian had gotten caught up in the 1959 Jackson County audit scandal, but was never charged or indicted for any wrongdoing.

Dunahoo also won, which was an upset as well. The Russell family was one of the most politically powerful in the state at the time. Notably, both Hoard and Dunahoo lost the Jackson County voting precinct of Cunningham (Pendergrass) where the county's "kingpin" bootlegger Cliff Park lived.

Quillian, upset at his loss to Hoard, resigned the solicitor general's position before the end of his term. On Monday, November 30, 1964, Hoard was sworn in a month early as solicitor general of the Piedmont Judicial Circuit.

He wasted no time. The next night after taking office, Hoard raided the Commerce DAV Club and arrested one person on bootlegging charges and confiscated several gambling machines. In the coming two weeks, he raided over a dozen other places in Jackson, Banks and Barrow counties for bootlegging and auto thefts. Around a dozen people, men and women, were charged.

Even before taking office, Hoard was preparing for the raids. He had given GBI agent Ronnie Angel $150 to make buys of illegal booze in the circuit. Angel said he made 54 buys before running out of money.

Hoard and Dunahoo further rattled the county's establishment in January 1965 when they upended the grand jury list. A grand jury had been appointed in December 1964 for the February 1965 court term by the group of jury commissioners.

Hoard and Dunahoo threw out that list, forced the resignation of the existing jury commissioners, named a new group, which then purged the grand jury and "petite jury" lists. Some of those purged were "leading citizens" in the county. In his court order, Dunahoo said there had been "irregularities" in the

December drawing of grand jury members.

Prior to February 1965, there hadn't been a single auto larceny case tried in Jackson County connected to the area's auto theft rings. Hoard blamed that on former Sheriff John B. Brooks who was himself a convicted car thief.

Hoard quickly tried to make up for that lack of aggressiveness. In the February 1965 grand jury term, just two months after he took office, Hoard got 76 indictments on auto theft charges.

It was one thing to get indictments, another to actually convict. When it came time for court in 1965, most of those charged were no-shows. The court asked the public to help find six of the defendants and Judge Dunahoo issued 27 bench warrants.

One tactic used to avoid trial would be for a defendant to show up without a lawyer and ask for a continuance multiple times.

Still, Hoard and Dunahoo persisted. Usually there were just two terms of court a year — February and August. Dunahoo added extra weeks in February, April, August, September and October in 1965 in a bid to try all the car theft cases Hoard was making.

But the going was slow. There were also a number of murder cases to try that year and by August 1965, only 10 of the 76 auto theft cases had been tried. Part of the problem, Hoard told the August grand jury, was a lack of funding to pay for jurors and other costs associated with so many cases.

Despite Hoard's efforts, the car thefts continued. By early 1966, following a "lull" in the fall of 1965, there was an up-tick in car theft activity. In January 1966, two stripped cars were found, one stolen from UGA that was owned by a man in Boston, Mass. It was found with bullet holes in it. Other cars were stolen that week, too, but not recovered.

In response, a group of Jackson and Banks County citizens organized "Citizens for Better Government" to address the crime issues. It partnered with the Commerce Kiwanis Club and 26 people from the group met with Gov. Carl Sanders to press for state help in cleaning up Northeast Georgia. The president of Roper Pump Company in Commerce also petitioned the governor for help in a letter.

Even as Hoard pressed his prosecutions, there were setbacks. In trials in February 1966, two men charged with auto thefts were found not guilty by juries. Judge Dunahoo issued a strong rebuke to jurors in comments from the bench:

"We have the very practical need to convict the guilty felon and not permit him to be freed on trivial technicalities. The people need to be protected from these criminals."

In July, a routine road check in Jackson County found a car filled with parts from a vehicle stolen in Madison County. Also that summer, six people, including some teens, were charged with auto theft in Banks County. Four pled guilty.

More stolen cars were found in Pendergrass that summer and a car owned by a local soldier was stolen from the parking lot of Maysville Baptist Church.

In September 1966, two teens were charged with stealing a car from the Jefferson Mills parking lot. It was found stripped and burned off the Brockton Road.

In October, a 1965 GTO was stolen from the Halloween Carnival at Jackson County High School in Braselton. It was found stripped off I-85. Among those arrested was the car owner's grandson. Another car stolen from a UGA student was found rammed into an embankment off Sandy Creek Road.

Even with Hoard's push and some help from citizens pressing for more state assistance, car thefts and bootlegging continued almost unabated in 1965-1966.

Hoard also found that punishing bootleggers wasn't easy. While a conviction on auto theft might mean jail time, bootlegging only carried a small fine, unless it involved moonshine and the feds were involved.

"Most of the people on the bootlegging circuit in the county expected to be caught and they paid a fine then they went back into business again," said former GBI agent Angel. "The expectation of being caught was just the cost of doing business."

Often, bootlegging cases would be dismissed, or not called for trial. Even if it was called for trial, juries would often not convict a bootlegger. Many citizens believed bootlegging and moonshining to be harmless, just a necessary part of life in a "dry" county.

But it was a big business in Northeast Georgia. Over a six-month period in 1966, state revenue agents found 1,735 moonshine stills and arrested 1,877 people. That was statewide, but much of it was concentrated in Northeast Georgia. At the time of his death in 1967, Hoard had made 130 cases against area bootleggers.

As Hoard began hitting local bootleggers in 1965 and 1966, the IRS started an anti-moonshine campaign via radio and television public service announcements in Atlanta that focused on the danger of drinking moonshine. Called "Operation Dry Up," the anti-moonshine campaign pointed out how lead salts from stills made their way into finished moonshine. The accumulation of lead could cause blindness and even death.

One of the side effects of that anti-moonshine campaign actually led to even a more poisonous moonshine mixture. The state's crackdown on stills and bootlegging in 1965-66 more than doubled the street price of illicit moonshine. That led some moonshine retailers in the Atlanta area to add Solox, a paint thinner, to moonshine being sold to the public. Atlanta officials worried that the move would lead to another rash of moonshine deaths as happened with some poisoned moonshine in the city in 1951 that killed over 40 people.

Silence and apathy from the area's decent citizens was something that frustrated Hoard as he began to prosecute local rackets. In 1965, soon after taking office, he issued a report to the grand jury that said he had to fight both the "criminal element" and the "respectable element" in his bid to close down bootleggers and car thieves. Hoard was particularly upset that 259 people, some of whom were county officials, had petitioned the court in 1965 to suspend the sentence of former Sheriff Brooks, who had been convicted in Fulton County for car theft.

"The respectable people who signed this request did not realize the implications of their conduct, that they were actually endorsing, indirectly, the criminal element in our county and state," Hoard said of that effort to help Brooks.

An editorial in *The Jackson Herald* in March 1965 asked, "Do the citizens want this county 'cleaned up' or do they really care?"

That sentiment was also expressed by another local editor after Hoard was killed.

"The people just haven't done a damn thing about it, that's the trouble," Albert Hardy, editor and owner of *The Commerce News* told the *Associated Press* in 1967.

Hardy knew the danger of focusing on local crime. In 1963, after *The News* had reported about local car thefts, eight of the newspaper's office windows were broken — an old car spring had been thrown through one of them. At the same time, members of the Commerce City Council received phone calls threatening to burn their houses down. The message was clear — silence was best.

Politics was also a problem. The area's illegal operations had become big business. To protect that, criminal ring-leaders donated a lot of money to local candidates who would pledge to turn a blind eye to their operations.

The *Associated Press* spoke to an unnamed local car thief who in 1967 told the reporter he had put $10,000 into one local campaign in 1964. Donations, bribery and stuffed ballot boxes to protect the "rackets" were not uncommon in that era.

W. DuBose

Jefferson Presbyterian Resigned to Acc... Easley, S. C.

...Bose will soon leave

...e years he has served
...church in Jefferson,
one a splendid work
...astorate, a commodi-
manse has been erect-
building has been re-
...bership of the church
Sunday school devel-
...regations have grown
...salary of the pastor
bled and the Master's
...

...is interested in the
own church, but he is
...e in a town and com-
thing that will benefit

...has indefatigable en-
...ever satisfied with his
always trying to find
...to do or to perform
greater efficiency. He
...reat worker, but has
...tting others to work

...he a worker, but he is
history and the Bible,
...up with current
quite an entertaining

...hese, however, he is a
...cher. His sermons not
...m the head, but from
...he is a man of God—
to do God's will.

A BIG HAUL

A Distillery Brought In Saturday Night By Officers. Found In Newtown District. Six Hundred Gallons Beer Destroyed.

A distillery and 600 gallons of beer.

Saturday night, in Newtown district, Sheriff Barber and Deputy Pendergrass captured this distillery and poured out 600 gallons of beer.

They had been given a tip just where the distillery was located, so Saturday night, far into the night, they went in search of it. In a quiet and careful manner they approached it. They were in hopes of finding men at work, but when they reached the factory of iniquity the fire had been pulled and the men flown. Evidently somewhere someone was on guard and notified the distillers of the approach of officers.

A 45-gallon distillery was in active operation. The distillery was taken into custody by the officers and before leaving they poured out about 600 gallons of beer, showing that the parties who operated the distillery intended to make a big run.

While the officers did not find the men at work in the distillery, yet they feel sure the other evidence is sufficient to convict the guilty ones. They have the evidence and the names of the parties at whom the evidence points, but at present they decline to divulge the names of the ones against whom cases will be made.

NINTH DISTRICT W IN STATE AG. IN

Third Annual G...

The third annual me... Agricultural High scho... was held last week in... Ninth district came out ...ers. and the fact ...as table in the light of the ...school for the year pr... ore. The district had ... girls to support the ...teams.

Early Monday mornin... delegation began to a... mobiles decorated with Georgia, the college colo... school at Clarkesville. ...ed every meeting and there was always a joll... ed mass of the Ninth... root and cheer for th... from their school. Esp... siastic were they at th... events — their yells b... louder and fuller of p... rest of the groups. Th... everywhere to be seen well-behaved and fine loo... ting everybody know... the Ninth district Ag and of it.

What They Di

Here's the rec... for ...ants from the Ninth in events and the places they final results as a school ... grand prize of the meet:

Debate: Henry Black... Blackwell.

Cooking: Esther Rope... Poultry: Ruth Garrison

Newspaper article from 1918 in *The Jackson Herald* about a raid on a large moonshine still in Jackson County.

62

A 1958 photo of an area moonshine still raided by law enforcement officials.

A 1962 raid of a bootlegging house in Pendergrass led to the arrest of Wes Smith (right). It was just one of many raids in the 1950s and early 1960s.

PICTURED HERE IS THE HULL of a 1962 Ford Galaxie found near Hoschton, Thursday by Federal Agents. No torch was used on the car, instead wrenches were used to disassemble it.

An article from 1963 reflects the huge rise in auto thefts that left hundreds of cars stripped in Jackson County.

The old Jackson County
Jail in Jefferson.

Convict Admits Killing In Jefferson, Saving Foster From Chair

S. Carolinan To Go Free In a Week

By Jack Nelson

FOSTER FLANKED BY HIS ATTORNEYS AND JACKSON SHERIFF

Foster's Loyal Lawyer Sacrificed and Won

By MARION GAINES

Integration Stirs NEA Floor Fight

By LEONARD BUDER

The July 5, 1958 front page of the *Atlanta Constitution* with a story about the sensational Drake murder case in Jefferson. The wrong man, James Foster (middle of the photo), was initially convicted for the murder of Jefferson businessman Charles Drake and sentenced to the electric chair. Floyd Hoard (far left) and James Horace Wood (second from left) defended Foster. In 1958, another man, Rocky Rothschild, confessed to the murder, saving Foster. The case garnered national attention and for a time, made Hoard and Wood celebrities. Wood would later defend two of Hoard's killers in the 1968 trials.

In a dramatic meeting on the lawn of the Jackson County Courthouse on July 8, 1958, Rocky Rothschild (right) embraced James Foster as Floyd Hoard (left) looked on. Rothschild confessed to murdering Charlie Drake in a 1956 robbery, a confession that saved Foster who had been wrongly convicted and sentenced to death. Hoard was one of Foster's court-appointed lawyers.

Judge Disbars Clinkscales in Directed Verdict

Ford Plant To Close For Week

Ford Motor Co. announced Thursday its Hapeville assembly plant will be closed for a week beginning Monday for "inventory adjustment."

The Hapeville plant currently employs some 1,400 people.

General Motors last month laid off about 900 men for an indefinite period at its Buick-Oldsmobile-Pontiac plant at Doraville.

6 PLANTS AFFECTED

The B-O-P plant is still employing more than 1,550 workers and plant officials said there are no plans for a further reduction of the work force.

Ford announced Thursday a layoff of about 6,200 workers will

"WE'LL APPEAL."
Maylon B. Clinkscales

Step Softly, Kennedy

Ex-Jurist Guilty of Misconduct

By FRANK WELLS
Constitution Staff Writer

JEFFERSON—Former Superior Court Judge Maylon B. Clinkscales Thursday was barred from the practice of law by a court-directed verdict of guilty to numerous charges of legal misconduct.

Judge F. Frederick Kennedy took the case under his own direction and ordered the jury to return a verdict of guilty on 13 charges of Clinkscales' misconduct. He directed a verdict of innocent on five others.

Five of the charges on which Clinkscales was found guilty linked his actions as judge with those of Marvin Pierce, Winder attorney, whose name was frequently mentioned as the case progressed.

WILL APPEAL

A front page story in the *Atlanta Constitution* in February 1961 tells of the disbarment of Jackson County Superior Court Judge Maylon Clinkscales. Clinkscales was found guilty on a variety of allegations of public corruption that came out of a 1959 audit of the Jackson County finances. Clinkscales had earlier been indicted on some of the charges, but was never tried. A local lawyer linked to Clinkscales' actions was also disbarred.

Sheriff Posts Bond In Tax Evasion Case

Jackson County Sheriff John B. Brooks, ha been released on $1,000 bond in connection with a federal income tax evasion complaint filed by the U. S. Internal Revenue Service in Atlanta.

The sheriff's attorney posted the bond before the U. S. District commissioner' office in Gainesville.

The complaint contented that Brooks owed $445.05 in federal income tax in 1953 and paid nothing. It also said Sheriff Brooks reported his income that year at $2,995, but that his income was $5,000.23.

U. S. District Commissioner Ross Arnold of Atlanta received the complaint against the sheriff. It accused Brooks of violating USC title section 26, 145B of the federal code.

Sheriff Brooks was re-nominated two weeks ago to another four year term in the Jackson County Democratic Primary.

Sheriff John B. Brooks (photo) was a looming figure in Jackson County for four decades. By the late 1950s, he began to have his own legal problems. In 1959, he was accused by the IRS of tax evasion (left). The year before, an *Atlanta Constitution* investigation found that he had not paid county property taxes for a number of years.

68

Brooks Posts $25,000 Bond In Fulton; Trial To Be Set In Early October Court

Commerce Tigers Lose Opener; Play Winder Fri.

The Commerce Tigers journey to Winder this Friday night to play the Bulldogs at 8:00 p.m. This is the second game of the season for both teams, with Winder defeating Central Gwinnett and Commerce losing to Stephens County in the first game.

Commerce dropped the opener to Stephens County by a 14-0 score. The Tigers had trouble in the first quarter with their defense, but they settled down and held the Indians scoreless in the second half. Stephens County scored in the first quarter and early in the second quarter, and from there on it was a defensive battle. Commerce was unable to sustain an offensive drive, losing the ball three times by fumbles and twice by intercepted passes. Also the Tigers had two punts blocked, so the defensive team had to work double duty.

Playing outstanding defensive ball for Commerce were Truman Allen and Donald Chandler at ends, Larry Pardue and Lewis Sanders at tackles, Mike McClure

Sheriff John B. Brooks of Jackson County posted a $25,000 bond in Fulton County Friday night following his arrest in Commerce. Jackson County Coroner Tom Conn arrested Brooks on a bench warrant from Fulton Superior Court.

The warrant charged Brooks and four Jackson Countians with being accessories-before-the-fact in connection with the theft of an automobile in Fulton County.

A Fulton County grand jury returned the indictments. Authorities kept the knowledge quiet until bench warrants could be issued and officers could drive to Jackson County, Sol. Gen. William Boyd said.

Sheriff Brooks is 53 years old and has been sheriff of Jackson County for 21 years.

A county coroner is the only official in a county allowed to arrest a sheriff. Friday afternoon at 5:30, Coroner Tom Conn of Commerce said he called Sheriff Brooks and asked him to "come to Commerce . . . that I had something to talk to him about."

Conn said when he called the sheriff he didn't tell him he had a bench warrant for his arrest. He said he has known the sheriff for 18 years. "I've been here (Commerce) for about 18 years,"

Conn said he knew the sheriff all that time.

Conn said when Sheriff Brooks arrived in Commerce he told the sheriff he had a bench warrant for his arrest. He said Brooks asked "for what?"

Conn said he read the warrant to the sheriff, charging him with being an accessory-before-the-fact to an auto larceny. "Then I told him I was turning him over to the GBI." Conn said GBI agents were present when the warrant was read.

Brooks was taken to Fulton County Jail where he posted a bond of $25,000 prior to midnight Friday, Fulton Deputy Sheriff Bob Poole said.

Sol. Gen. William Boyd said Saturday he will "try the sheriff as soon as possible." He said the superior court docket for September is filled so he will have to schedule the case for early October. Brooks' counsel is John Darsey of Commerce.

In 1963, Jackson County Sheriff John B. Brooks was arrested and convicted of auto theft. Brooks had been sheriff since 1943 and was also involved in bootlegging in the county. Brooks finished out his term of office and didn't go to prison until 1965. At the time, a lot of "leading citizens" in the county petitioned the court to not send Brooks to jail, a move that angered new Solicitor General Floyd Hoard.

LANDRUM EDGES MILLER

Dunahoo, Hoard Get Nominations

A total of 4,435 Jackson Countians went to the polls last Wednesday and played a decisive role in the results of several races in the State Democratic Primary.

One run-off will be required. Neither incumbent Allen Chappell nor leading contender Alpha A. Fowler received a majority in the four-man race for Public Service Commissioner, and a run-off between the two will be held on September 23.

The office of the Secretary of State has yet to compile the complete returns of the Statewide race, but the latest totals showed Chappell leading Fowler by a vote of 125,064 to 96,921.

Incumbent 9th District Congressman Phil Landrum ran into stiffer opposition than expected but again obtained the Democratic nomination by receiving 28,055 votes throughout the district. Runner-up Zell Miller polled 22,741 votes, while Franklyn "Buckeye" Stone Uhl received 2,611 votes.

Congressman Landrum is expected to receive opposition in the November General Election from Republican Jack Prince, who had no primary opposition.

Dr. J. Albert Minish was unopposed for the State Senator from the 48th District.

In the races for Judge and Solicitor General of the Piedmont Judicial Circuit, Mark Dunahoo upset incumbent Judge Richard B. Russell III and Jefferson attorney Floyd Hoard defeated present Solicitor General Alfred Quillian. Dunahoo had a total of 5,106 votes to 4,665 for Russell, while Hoard collected 5,197 votes to 4,823 for Quillian.

The break-down, by counties, in the Piedmont Judicial Circuit races is as follows:

Judge: Banks County, Dunahoo 897, Russell 656; Jackson County, Dunahoo 2,457, Russell 1,869; Barrow County, Dunahoo 1,762, Russell 2,140.

Solicitor: Banks County, Hoard 905, Quillian 873; Jackson County, Hoard 2,845, Quillian 1,507; Barrow County, Hoard 1,447, Quillian 2,443.

Results of Justice of the Peace and Constable races throughout Jackson County were as follows:

Jefferson District: Talmadge Perry defeated Thomas B. Kinsey for JP; J. B. Alexander was elected Constable.

Harrisburg District: Lester Maul-

and Jack Carlan were elected Constables.

Newtown District: John W. Tolbert was elected JP; W. M. Tolbert was elected Constable.

Center District: Olin Farmer was elected JP; no candidate for Constable.

Attica District: John T. Hale was elected JP; W. R. Nixon defeated C. H. Bullock for Constable position No. 1, and J. B. Huntsinger was elected to fill the other Constable post.

Redstone District: Joe Baerne was elected JP; Bennie W. Compton and F. L. Nixon were elected Constables.

Randolph District: H. W. Summerour was elected JP; Ralph B. Phillips and Bartow Hall were elected Constables.

Hoschton District: A. J. Reynolds was elected JP; W. A. Heflin was elected Constable.

Porters District: J. M. Davenport was elected JP; J. T. Gunter defeated J. H. White for Constable

position No. 1, and Otis H. McNeal was elected to fill the other Constable post.

Talmo District: Ted Cook was elected JP; J. C. Sosebee Sr. was elected Constable.

Cunningham District: Homer McDonald was elected JP; Gerald Sanders was elected Constable.

Millers District: F. R. Wilson was elected JP; no candidate for Constable.

Wilson District: T. S. Ray was elected JP; Sam Crane was elected Constable.

THREE PERSONS were killed near Commerce on U. S. 441 Saturday, September 12, when their car was literally demolished by a tractor-trailer. State Patrolmen listed the victims as Lloyd Meeks of Cornelia, Richard T. Harris, route 2, Danielsville, and J. P. Hubbard of route one, Maysville. Meeks and Harris were killed instantly and Hubbard was dead on arrival at BJC Hospital. According to officers the three were in a 1956 Chevrolet which was in collision with a tractor-trailer driven by Ralph Bentley of Anniston. He was only slightly injured, but was hospitalized for observation. —Photo by Sib Alexander.

Watershed Group Reelects Officers

All officers were reelected for another year at the Middle Oco-

The officers are Smith Bridges, president; Tom Blackstock, vice

application for planning was approved in the Spring. The Water-

---

In 1964, Jefferson attorney Floyd Hoard was elected solicitor general of the Piedmont Judicial Circuit. He had run on a reform campaign to clean up the circuit, which includes Jackson County. He ousted the incumbent in the election and along with new judge Mark Dunahoo, began a crusade against car thieves and bootleggers in the circuit.

Floyd "Fuzzy" Hoard
1965

Floyd Hoard with son Richard "Dickey" and daughter Peggy Jean.

Floyd Hoard

Andrew Clifford Park in an undated photo. Park would be convicted in 1968 of having solicited and paid for the murder of Solicitor General Floyd Hoard.

Cliff Park with wife Mae Lou (left) and daughter Diane in 1971.

Cliff Park with wife Mae Lou.

Jury Indicts Cliff Park

The Grand Jury returned two true bills against Andrew Cliff Park, of Pendergrass, this week on liquor violation charges. Park, referred to by federal agents in a bootlegging", was indicted for "a king-pin of Northeast Georgia bootlegging55, was indicted for possessing more than one quart of tax paid liquor in a dry county. The second indictment was for transporting more than one quart of tax paid liquor in a dry county.

The prosecutors on both indictments were Revenue Agents Isaac Davis and John Pardue.

Born in 1891, Cliff Park had a long history of legal entanglement from moonshining and bootlegging dating back to 1916. For the most part, he avoided convictions until the early 1960s when federal charges sent him to prison for a year. In this news article from 1959, Park was indicted by a local grand jury for bootlegging. The article refers to Park as a "king-pin" of Northeast Georgia bootleggers. The outcome of that 1959 indictment is unclear.

76

Jackson County Sheriff L. G. "Snuffy" Perry became a major part of the story of the murder of Floyd Hoard. Above, Perry stands on the porch of the old Jackson County Jail with some of the beer confiscated from Hoard's May 1967 raid on Cliff Park's bootlegging operation. At right, Perry and a deputy padlock a bootlegging house in 1966. Perry would be forced out of the Hoard investigation in the fall of 1967.

On the morning of August 7, 1967, Solicitor General Floyd Hoard was murdered when 10 sticks of dynamite went off in his car in front of his home outside of Jefferson. Hoard died at the scene. The blast made national headlines and brought in a large number of state and federal officers to investigate the assassination.

The blast that killed Floyd Hoard left his car mangled. The dynamite had been place on a strut on the left side of the car (below).

Devoted to the Progress of Jackson County

The Jackson Herald

10c PER COPY · OFFICIAL ORGAN OF JACKSON COUNTY · JEFFERSON, GEORGIA, JACKSON COUNTY 30549 · Wednesday, August 9, 1967

EADS 'THAT SOUND GOOD' BEING FOLLOWED UP
N GANGLAND-STYLE KILLING OF FLOYD HOARD

SOL. GEN. FLOYD HOARD

Maddox Sends In More State Officers

No Successor To Mr. Hoard Appointed Yet

JHS Grid Season To Open Aug. 25

An Editorial

They killed Floyd Hoard.

Or was it "they"?

Did we in Jackson County by our apathy, our ignorance, our fear, our failure to lend law enforcement and the courts our full-hearted support help create a climate which led to this heinous crime?

'...He Had Counted The Cost'

County Reels From Shock

DEATH CAR

The front page two days after the murder with the masthead in mourning black. Floyd Hoard had been editor of *The Jackson Herald* for a short time in 1959-1960 and had spoken out against the county's lawlessness in his writings.

80

Georgia, JACKSON County.

IN THE SUPERIOR COURT OF SAID COUNTY

The Grand Jurors selected, chosen and sworn for the County of _Jackson_ , to-wit:

1. Allen S. Phillips .... FOREMAN
2. Hal M. Nix
3. William Wright
4. P. J. Roberts Jr.
5. Harold J. Wardlaw
6. Forrest L. Hagan
7. Quillian Smith
8. S. R. Blackstock
9. John Q. White
10. Arthur W. Riddle
11. W. W. Daniel
12. Grady Smith
13. Gus Johnson
14. Hoyt Harbin
15. J. V. Bright
16. Hoyt Purcell
17. Hoyt Fleming
18. Joseph O. Waters Sr.
19. Jack J. Ward
20. Garnett L. Martin
21. Elmon Farmer
22. Joshua F. Pirkle
23.

in the name and behalf of the citizens of Georgia, charge and accuse

A. C. (Cliff) Park, George Douglas Pinion, Lloyd George Seay, George Iras Worley, and John Hyman Blackwell of the County and State aforesaid, with the offense of _____ Murder _____

for that the said A. C. (Cliff) Park, George Douglas Pinion, Lloyd George Seay, George Iras Worley, John Hyman Blackwell

on the _7_ day of _August_ , in the year of our Lord Nineteen Hundred and _sixty-seven_

in the County aforesaid, did then and there unlawfully with force and arms unlawfully, feloniously, and with malice aforethought kill and murder Floyd G. Hoard with, by the use of and by explosion of dynamite, powder, nitroglycerine and other explosive substance, compound and like device, thereby inflicting upon Floyd G. Hoard a mortal wound and and mortal wounds from which the said Floyd G. Hoard then and there died,

This is the December 1967 indictment by the Jackson County Grand Jury of the five men accused of having murdered Floyd Hoard. The grand jury had been slated to meet the morning of Hoard's murder. That was postponed until October 1967 when it began investigating the crime and officials connected to the county's legacy of corruption.

81

DOUGLAS PINION

LLOYD GEORGE SEAY
Defendant, State Witness

These are four of the five men convicted in January 1968 for the murder of Floyd Hoard. Doug Pinion (upper left) was associated with Cliff Park and was the go-between with Lloyd Seay (upper right) in soliciting the murder. John Blackwell (lower left) placed the bomb in Hoard's car and George Worley (lower right) showed Seay and Blackwell where Hoard lived.

J. H. BLACKWELL
Defendant, State Witness

GEORGE WORLEY

A. C. "Cliff" Park was convicted on January 10, 1968 as the mastermind who put in motion the events that led to the murder of Floyd Hoard. Park had his first conviction overturned, but was convicted a second time in 1969. He appealed the second verdict and was in and out of prison. He died in prison in 1978.

Judge Mark Dunahoo (left) was elected in 1964 along with Floyd Hoard on a clean-up campaign. Dunahoo presided over the 1968 trials of those convicted of Hoard's murder. He is shown here with Luther Hames (right), the prosecutor from Cobb County who helped prosecute the five men in the murder.

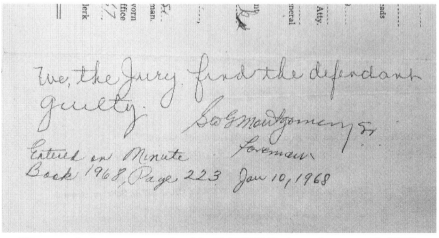

The conviction paperwork of A. C. "Cliff" Park on January 10, 1968 signed by the foreman of the jury, George Montgomery, Sr.

Peggy Hoard Tried To Save Father

JEFFERSON, Ga. — Peggy Jean Hoard, 16, daughter of slain Prosecutor Floyd Hoard, leaves the Jackson County, Ga., courthouse Wednesday after testifying that she gave artificial resuscitation to her father shortly after he was fatally wounded in a bomb blast last August. Miss Hoard testified in the Jefferson, Ga., trial of A. C. Park, who is accused of conspiring with four other men to kill Hoard by bombing his auto. (AP Wirephoto)

One of those who testified early in the trials was Floyd Hoard's daughter, Peggy Jean. This *Associated Press* photo of her leaving the courthouse was published in newspapers all across the nation.

A. C. "Cliff" Park (above) was convicted twice for the murder of Floyd Hoard. These photos were taken outside the Jackson County Courthouse during those trials.

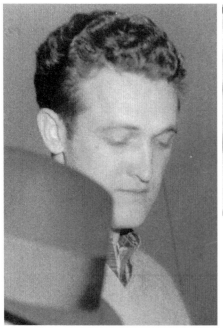

The two key witnesses in the murder case were John H. Blackwell (left) and Lloyd Seay (right) who confessed to the killing and testified against the others. Both got life sentences for their cooperation.

SOLICITORS, GBI — Sol. Gen. G. Wesley Channell (left) and Sol. Gen Emeritus Luther Hames (next on front) are leading the prosecution of defendants on trial in the Floyd Hoard murder case. With them are three GBI officials, Major Barney Ragsdale (extreme right, front) Sgt. R. E. Hightower (left, rear) and Capt. J. E. Carnes (right, rear), head of the GBI investgation team.

WITNESS — Ronald Angel (above) GBI agent who did extensive work on the Hoard murder case has spent much time on the stand during the trials.

Some of the key law enforcement officials involved in the Floyd Hoard murder case are shown in this 1968 photo. Georgia Bureau of Investigation agent Ronnie Angel (right) was the key person in the arrest and conviction of those responsible for Hoard's murder. Angel had worked with Hoard in his crusade against the area's bootleggers and car thieves.

GBI agent R. J. Cleghorn (right) was another key player in the Hoard murder investigation. Cleghorn was head of the GBI office in Gainesville and had worked with Hoard in the May 1967 raid on Cliff Park's bootlegging establishment. Cleghorn had warned Hoard against telling Jackson County Sheriff L. G. "Snuffy" Perry (left) about the raid fearing that Perry would tip off Park in advance.

1927   1967

FLOYD G. HOARD
SOLICITOR GENERAL OF THE PIEDMONT JUDICIAL CIRCUIT
HOARD WAS KILLED BY A CAR BOMB
AUGUST 7, 1967, WHILE AGGRESSIVELY
PROSECUTING ORGANIZED CRIME
WITHIN THE CIRCUIT

"WE NOW REALIZE THAT THE PRESERVER OF LAW
AND ORDER IS COURAGE AND THAT FEAR AND
INACTIVITY IN THE FACE OF THREATS AND GROWING
CRIME CAN ONLY LEAD US TO MORAL DECAY."
FLOYD G. HOARD

ERECTED WITH GRATITUDE BY THE CITIZENS
OF BANKS, BARROW, AND JACKSON COUNTIES
APRIL 19, 1992

Monument to Floyd "Fuzzy" Hoard on the grounds of the Historic Jackson County Courthouse in Jefferson.

9.
The Park Raid

In early 1967, after two years of hitting various bootleggers and auto thieves in the Piedmont Judicial Circuit, Solicitor General Floyd Hoard decided to raid Cliff Park's Pendergrass operation in a bid to close it down once and for all.

Exactly why he decided to take the action at that time and not earlier is unclear. Former GBI agent Ronnie Angel said Hoard told him that his two teenage kids would come home from school talking about how open the Park operation was running and that he had heard the joke about needing cops to direct traffic at Park's business.

"I've listened to the kids' stories and everywhere I go people say, 'Why don't you do something about it?' so I'm finally going to do something about it," Angel recalled Hoard saying leading up to his plans to raid Park.

Hoard may have been feeling some political pressure by then, too. Hoard and Judge Mark Dunahoo had run on a reform and clean-up the circuit platform in 1964. There would be another election in 1968.

Whatever the reasons, Hoard brought in the GBI and state revenue agents in the spring of 1967 to help with the Park probe, but he didn't tell Jackson County Sheriff L. G. "Snuffy" Perry. Perry had been elected in 1964 at the same time as Hoard and Dunahoo. But Hoard had been warned by a local GBI agent to keep the sheriff out of the loop lest Park get wind of what was going on.

Keeping raids silent wasn't easy in a small town where everyone seemed to know everyone else's business. One Jefferson woman who worked as a teenage waitress at Marlow's Café, the local Jefferson coffee hangout for court and law officials, recalled that Hoard would often come into the restaurant in the afternoons carrying his briefcase and sit in the first booth. His brother-in-law, Jefferson Police Chief Albert Westmoreland, was also a regular, along with other lawyers and county officials. She said it was common for the officials to discuss impending raids as they sipped their coffee.

"We knew about some of the upcoming raids" from overhearing the conversations, she said.

Imogene Hoard remembers that 40-50 state agents gathered at their rural house after dark one night to plan the raids on Park and his associates in the spring of 1967. They turned off their car lights at they drove up the Hoards' long driveway, she said. Undercover law enforcement officers like Angel made numerous purchases of illegal booze to help Hoard get warrants for the raid and a court order to padlock Park's operations. Angel said he made 14 buys at Park's house and 10 at Park's allied "yellow house" between April 29 and May 5, 1967.

The big raid of Park's operation was scheduled for Saturday afternoon, May 6, 1967. But there was the question about the sheriff. Hoard and Perry had what appeared to be a difficult relationship. There was a story at the time — perhaps just rumor — that Perry and Hoard had a meeting at which Perry told the solicitor general, "You do the prosecuting and I'll do the policing."

Whatever the situation, agent Angel said there "appeared to be a rift" between the two officials. At the time, sheriffs were very powerful under the old county unit system in the state and very protective of their "turf."

Jackson County was a little different. Under an executive order from Governor Lester Maddox, the Georgia Bureau of Investigation was allowed to come into Jackson County without an invitation from the local sheriff, the only county in the state where that was allowed. The governor signed the order in an effort to clean up the auto theft problem in Jackson County. That order was later codified by a local referendum in 1971. Today, Jackson County remains the only county in Georgia where the GBI has full access without local law enforcement consent.

Hoard didn't fully trust Perry, but he felt that they had to work together. A few evenings before the May 1967 raid, Hoard called GBI agent R. J. Cleghorn, Angel's boss, and asked him to come to his house. The two men took a ride in Hoard's pickup truck.

"I think I ought to tell the sheriff," Cleghorn later recalled Hoard saying about the impending raid.

Cleghorn replied, "Solicitor, you are the one handling the raid... if you want to tell the sheriff, you tell him." Cleghorn pointed out that if Park got word of the raid, it would hurt the effort to shut him down.

"The fine you get off of a man like that is not a drop in the bucket," Cleghorn told Hoard that night as they drove around the county. "The merchandise you take away from him is where you tear him up."

At some point that Wednesday or Thursday in early May 1967, Hoard told Sheriff Perry of the Park raid planned for Saturday afternoon. On Thursday night before the raid, Hoard went to Cleghorn's GBI office in Gainesville to draw up the warrants. While he was there, he asked Cleghorn to call agent Angel and have him go make buys at both the "yellow house" and Park's garage.

A little while later, Angel showed up at Cleghorn's office with some beer and whiskey he'd bought from Park. Hoard, sitting behind the desk, reached over to the booze and said, "That means everything to me. You all don't know what that does mean to me."

Cleghorn said he knew exactly what Hoard meant.

"You've told the sheriff and you thought (Angel) wouldn't buy anything — (they) wouldn't sell him nothing."

"That's exactly right," Hoard replied.

For a moment, Hoard thought the raid had been kept a secret and that he could trust Perry. That confidence lasted barely 24 hours. On Friday night before the planned raid, agent Angel was watching the Park operation from nearby. At about 10 p.m., he went into Park's bootlegging garage to make another buy. There, he saw a large truck backed up and men loading up the booze from Park's place.

Angel quickly drove to a pay phone at I-85 and called Cleghorn to alert him to the movement. Park has obviously been tipped off about the raid planned for the following day.

Cleghorn then called Hoard, who was taking a bath.

"I need to talk to him right quick," Cleghorn told Hoard's wife, Imogene, who had answered the phone.

Hoard got out of the bath and when he heard what Angel had seen, told Cleghorn to meet him in Pendergrass.

Cleghorn, Angel and another GBI agent were waiting near Park's house when Hoard arrived. He had Sheriff Perry with him and a local state revenue agent. The revenue agent didn't want to be seen, so he lay down in a car and Angel drove him down the road 200 feet and left him there to hide.

The raid scheduled for the following day had been blown, so Hoard decided to go ahead and do the raid that night. Hoard, Perry and Cleghorn went to

Park's house, but found it locked up.

"I guess we'll have to wait until morning," Cleghorn later quoted Sheriff Perry as saying. "Everything's locked up, we can't get nobody to the door."

Cleghorn said he had a key — an ax in the trunk of his car.

The three discussed what to do and eventually, Hoard and the sheriff went back a second time to Park's house. A few minutes later, they drove out with Park in the car and took him to jail in Jefferson.

"We hauled beer all night," Cleghorn said when he testified in court about that raid.

A total of 12 places across the county were hit and 14 people, including Park, were arrested on a total of 53 charges. There was $21,700 worth of booze confiscated, 31 cases of whiskey and 2,254 cases of beer. Some of the booze was found in an old "meat house" behind Park's home. Of those charged, 13 posted a $500 bond and were released from jail. Park was required to post a "professional" bond.

But they didn't get all of the beer. One of those arrested got out of jail the next day and returned to Park's house where he got about 40 cases of beer from a "little old car" that was hidden. He took it to the "yellow house" and was back in business Saturday night. Law enforcement officials went back on Sunday and arrested him again, confiscating the 30 cases of beer he had left.

A front page photo in *The Jackson Herald* that week shows the beer stacked high on the front porch at the old county jail with Sheriff Perry standing in front.

On May 23, 1967, a court order to padlock Park's various locations was issued by Judge Dunahoo. Another bootlegger, an associate of Park, attempted to claim the beer was his in a bid to get it back and keep it from being destroyed, but Dunahoo denied his motion.

Park later pled guilty and paid a $4,500 fine in addition to the loss of his booze. He also paid the fines of two associates who had been charged for a total of $6,300.

Agent Angel believes that padlock order was what put into motion Park's plan to have Hoard killed. Getting arrested and paying a fine was one thing — having seven or eight locations padlocked would put Park out of business.

"This time Hoard petitioned the court for padlocking and I think that was the beginning of (Park's) decision to kill Hoard," Angel said.

But Sheriff Perry never carried out the court order to padlock Park's businesses. That lack of action became a huge issue for Perry after Hoard was killed.

Hoard was aware that he was making enemies with his crackdown on local crime rackets. Sometime around 1966, he began to carry a gun. The Barrow County sheriff recalled that Hoard had indicated to him the Saturday before the murder that he was in danger, but hadn't shared any details. Hoard also told an old college friend in July 1967 that an informant had told him, "You are fooling with some people who will kill you."

Hoard's brother, Joe, recalled that Floyd had asked him what he could do to stop his car from being bombed. Joe suggested that he put Scotch tape on the hood and check it every day to see if it had been broken. Hoard didn't follow that suggestion on the morning of August 7, 1967.

10.
The Murder Plot

In June 1967, just after Piedmont Judicial Circuit Solicitor General Floyd Hoard had led a major raid of Jackson County bootlegging operations and gotten a padlock order from the court, "kingpin" bootlegger Cliff Park sought his revenge.

Douglas Pinion, 40, who had worked for Park since 1965, approached fellow bootlegger Lloyd Seay, 24, of Dawson County and asked him if he wanted to make some "easy money." Seay said he was interested.

Pinion had long circulated in Jackson County's criminal underworld. In the mid-1950s, he got into a fight with Commerce's A. D. Allen and Pinion's father swore out warrants against Allen. Despite that, Pinion continued to be a part of Allen's circle of associates, as well as being part of Park's bootlegging operations. The criminal organizations run by Park and Allen did have some overlap, although they mostly stayed out of each other's way.

According to Jefferson native Gus Johnson, Pinion was well-known in the community and had a lot of friends.

"Everybody knew Doug," Johnson said. "He was more or less a driver (hauling liquor). It was well-known he was running liquor."

Former bootlegger Troy Lee Griffith echoed that.

"Everybody liked old Doug. He and TR hauled white liquor to Atlanta for Old Man Cliff. They didn't keep it a secret they was wheeling and dealing with moonshine. They wanted it to get out that they was 'the man.'"

For his part, Seay came into bootlegging and the criminal world naturally.

His uncle, Carl Lloyd Seay, was a famous Georgia bootlegger and early race car driver from Dawsonville who had been shot to death in 1941 by a cousin over a moonshine dispute. Seay's father, Jim, was also a Dawson County moonshiner who was also shot in that 1941 dispute, but survived.

"Jim Seay out of Dawsonville was Old Man Cliff's right hand man when it come to making liquor," Griffith recalled. "Old Man Cliff just took part of it, but he put the money up for it. He (Jim) was Lloyd Seay's daddy, so that's how that come about."

As a child, Seay had lived in Pendergrass for a while, about a mile from Park's house. The younger Seay had dropped out of school in the 10th grade and was in and out of trouble in Dawson County, often riding around the town square with other thugs, daring local law enforcement officers to stop them.

In a 1977 interview with the *Atlanta Constitution*, Seay said that as a kid, he began hauling sugar to a liquor still on a sled drawn by mules. Later, he began running moonshine from Dawson County to Atlanta. Seay had also served time in the Jackson County "chain-gang" for an assault and battery in Lumpkin County in 1963.

Pinion told Seay in June 1967 that to make some "easy money," he "wanted a man done away with." He said it was Hoard, the crusading prosecutor. During the conversation, Pinion referenced "the Old Man," a nickname used to refer to the 76-year-old Park, as wanting Hoard killed.

Pinion offered Seay $5,000 to do the murder and said it would be best if he did it on the road with a shotgun as Hoard was driving home from work. Seay told Pinion he wasn't interested in doing it himself, but would try to find someone who would.

Seay then approached George Worley, 40, of Commerce about the killing, but apparently didn't tell him at first who the target would be. Worley was another longtime associate of Allen and had previous criminal problems, including a 1960 indictment related to car theft. Worley, a veteran of the Air Force, had also been indicted in 1959, along with two men from Mississippi and Arkansas, for breaking into the Commerce Veterans Home. Worley was reportedly associated with "Rocky" Rothschild, who had confessed to the 1956 murder of Charles Drake in Jefferson. According to former moonshiner Troy Lee Griffith, Worley was a frequent poker player with Allen. Worley told Seay that he wanted $7,500 to do the hit.

After Worley told Seay his price for getting rid of Hoard, Seay went back to

Pinion and told him he had found someone to do the job, but it would take more money. Pinion told Park Worley's price, but Park refused to pay more than $5,000.

Pinion relayed Park's message to Seay and said that he would add $500 to the payment from his own pocket. Seay then went back to Worley with the offer of $5,500. Worley was reportedly reluctant to do it, but said he would go ahead.

Seay also asked fellow bootlegger John H. Blackwell, 23, of Pickens County, if he had the nerve to kill someone. Seay and Blackwell had been making moonshine together in Dawson County for a few months.

Tall and lanky with curly black hair, Blackwell had been kicked out of the military after he got caught running moonshine while home on leave. Blackwell said he didn't have the nerve to kill anyone, but was asked by Seay to join the hit operation anyway.

Seay later said he had approached four people about doing the hit, but it's not known who all the others were. One area hit-man reportedly turned down assassinating Hoard because of the likelihood of a law enforcement backlash.

In his book, *"Rock Solid, In His Own Words,"* Billy Stonewall Birt says that his hit-man father, Billy Sunday Birt of Winder, was asked to assassinate Hoard, but declined and also refused to sell his supply of dynamite to those planning to kill Hoard.

Stonewall Birt says that his father sent word to Park through a Barrow County bootlegger that killing Hoard was "the dumbest thing he'd ever heard of."

On August 3, 1967, Seay, Blackwell and Worley met at the Firebird restaurant on I-85 in Banks County near Commerce and drove up I-85 to Anderson, S.C. Blackwell went into Freeman's Grocery, a one-room store operated by what he later said was an "older" woman, and bought 10 sticks of dynamite, five blasting caps and four bottles of beer. He used the name "Harold Smith" when he signed the receipt and told the woman the dynamite was going to be used for "well-drilling." The dynamite cost about $9 or $10, Blackwell later recalled.

When he got back to the car, Blackwell couldn't find an opener for the beer he had bought, so the trio stopped at a gas station on I-85 to borrow a bottle opener before driving back to Commerce. Worley went home while Seay and Blackwell headed back to Dawson County. Seay reportedly had his wife hide the dynamite under the kitchen sink.

On August 5, a Saturday, Seay showed Blackwell how to connect the blasting caps to the coil of an automobile at the Seay home in Dawsonville. Officers later found three dynamite caps where Blackwell had practiced doing the job.

On the night of August 6, Seay met Blackwell and driving Seay's mother's white 1964 car, went to Commerce where they picked up Worley around 10 p.m. With Seay driving, Worley showed the other two men Hoard's rural house on the Brockton Road near Jefferson.

The Hoard family had lived in downtown Jefferson for a while in the 1950s, but eventually bought a house on some acreage about three miles outside of town. The rural house stood on a slight hill in a grove of hardwood trees with a large open field in the front.

Seay reportedly told Blackwell "the man (Park) wanted it done that night before he (Hoard) went to court on Monday."

The three drove by Hoard's house the first time around 11 p.m. to midnight, but were confused at first about which house was Hoard's. They parked on a side road and Blackwell approached Hoard's house the first time to see if his car was there. He came back and told the others the car wasn't there because he didn't "want to go through with it." The group drove around some more, then between 12 and 1 a.m. returned.

While Blackwell and Worley used some black electrical tape to bundle the 10 sticks of dynamite together on the side of a nearby dirt road, Seay went to find Pinion to see if Hoard had traded cars. Pinion wasn't home and Seay then went to Hoard's yard to confirm the prosecutor's green car with a special radio antenna was parked there. It was.

Meanwhile, Worley punctured the center stick of dynamite on one end after the bundle had been taped together. Carrying the dynamite and one blasting cap, Blackwell, who had been drinking beer and popping pills that Sunday afternoon, took the bundle and approached Hoard's house twice before putting the dynamite under the hood. He said later he thought he was along for the operation that night to be a lookout, but at some point, consented to plant the bomb.

Hoard's dogs began barking as Blackwell tried to cross the large field in front of Hoard's house from the west, but it turned out they were on the backside of the house barking at something in the woods. Blackwell then approached the house from the east side. On a nearby hill, workers were catching chickens in a poultry house and loading them into trucks headed to area processing plants.

Wearing brown cotton gloves, Blackwell raised the hood on the car and groping in the semi-darkness — there was a yard light on a pole in the front yard — attached one wire of the blasting cap to the ignition coil. Taking a knife, he then "skinned" about two inches of rubber off of a wire or metal bar and wrapped the other wire of the blasting cap around the exposed metal for the ground. After inserting the blasting cap into the dynamite, Blackwell laid the bundle of explosives sideways on a support bar between the motor and left front fender, not far from the firewall and steering column on the driver's side.

Worley and Seay waited in the vehicle on a nearby dirt road as Blackwell put the explosives in place. After the bomb was planted, Blackwell returned to the others, telling Worley and Seay, "It's done." The three then drove to a nearby bridge and threw out Blackwell's shoes and gloves.

They took Worley to his home in Commerce, then Seay and Blackwell drove the rest of the night down to the town of Wrightsville in South Georgia, arriving around 8 a.m. There, they went to a local restaurant to meet with two bootleggers, the Powell brothers.

They didn't stay long — perhaps an hour — then drove back to Dawson County, hearing of Hoard's murder on the radio along the way. During the drive back, Seay told Blackwell to take off his shirt and throw it out the window, just in case it had any dynamite residue on it.

According to Griffith, who later married Seay's ex-wife Betty, when Seay arrived back home in Dawsonville, he began to cry. Betty, who by that point had figured out the real use for the dynamite she'd been asked to hide under the sink, reportedly told Seay, "Y'all done made a big mistake with what ya'll have done."

Several days later, Pinion brought $5,500 ($41,200 in 2018 dollars) to Seay, throwing the cash on a bed, then turned and walked away without saying anything. Seay called Worley to come get his share, then divided it out: $2,000 to himself, $2,000 to Worley and $1,500 to Blackwell. Blackwell gave $800 back to buy a 1958 car from Seay.

Hoard had been at his office in Jefferson late that Sunday night before his murder, spending part of the time showing his unfinished new office to Rep. James Paris of Winder, a fellow attorney and friend. When he came home around 11 p.m., he and wife Imogene checked on a water leak in the chicken house in the back, then returned to the house to wait on son "Dickey" to come home from a late movie. He got home around midnight and the family soon turned in for the night.

Hoard didn't say much over the years about any threats he had received, at least not to Imogene.

"He didn't want to upset me," she said.

She did overhear one conversation that might have been indicative of the kinds of threats her husband was getting: One summer evening, three men from Barrow County came to their house, she recalled, and stood outside talking to Hoard in the front yard. When he came back into the house, Hoard called the sheriff's office and asked that the three men be stopped and questioned. One of them had told Hoard, "Your wife will come home someday and see you nailed to the front door."

On the morning of August 7, 1967, the 40-year-old Hoard was slated to go to the Jackson County Courthouse where Superior Court was to begin with the grand jury meeting.

At home on that Monday morning were Imogene, 14-year-old "Dickey" and 16-year-old daughter, Peggy Jean. The other two daughters, Claudine and Vivian, were visiting an aunt for the weekend.

"Where are my girls?" Hoard had asked Imogene about the two younger kids the Friday before. Told they were spending the weekend away, he said, "Oh, I didn't get to tell them bye."

Officially, Hoard's agenda for that Monday was relatively routine, but some later speculated that he might have had a secret agenda to take to the grand jury. The May padlock order against Park's operations had not been carried out by Sheriff L. G. "Snuffy" Perry and some thought Hoard might have planned to take that to the grand jury for action.

The events of that Monday morning could have been different, too. Peggy Jean and her mother had discussed swapping vehicles that Monday so that Peggy Jean could use her dad's car to take a driving license test rather than in the family station wagon. Her dad's car had an automatic transmission while the other car didn't.

But Imogene said her husband's car had a police radio in it and that he might need it for work. And he had his paperwork in the car for that morning's court. They decided they would meet later in the day in town to swap cars for the driving test.

During the night of August 6, the Hoards' dogs barked some, family members later recalled, but that wasn't too unusual. A neighbor later said her dogs barked that night, too.

11.
"Who Would Have Done This?"

As Piedmont Judicial Circuit Solicitor General Floyd Hoard prepared to leave home for the courthouse on the morning of Aug. 7, 1967, he stopped in the house's foyer.

"He hugged me. He kissed me. He said, 'Don't ever forget how much I love you,'" Hoard's wife Imogene recalled. "I lived on that (memory) for a long time."

At 7:25 a.m., Hoard walked out the door of his green, wood frame house, which stood about 100 yards from the road on a hill amid a grove of hardwood trees. His car was parked facing the front door of the house, about 50 ft. away; the right rear was close to one of the trees in the front yard. He put the key in the ignition of his green 1966 Ford Galaxy 500 and turned the switch.

The explosion was immediate. The 10 sticks of dynamite shattered the front windows of the Hoard home and was heard in Jefferson three miles away and in the community of Nicholson farther to the east. Pieces of the car were blown 70 ft. away.

"We found some pieces of the vehicle on the opposite side of the house," recalled former GBI agent Cecil Callaway about the power of the blast.

The force of the explosion hit the driver's side hardest, blowing Hoard out of the driver's seat into the backseat. His shattered legs were draped over the front seat and a large piece of the dashboard lay across the midsection of his body. Peggy Jean jumped out of bed. Her room was on the front of the house, closest to the blast, and two large windows were shattered.

"You could hear glass, or you heard the front windows to the house just collapse," she said in court later. "It was just a frightening experience."

She ran to the smoking car where she tried to save her father's life with mouth-to-mouth resuscitation.

"He mumbled and he breathed a few times," she was quoted in that week's *Jackson Herald.* "I tried to bring him back."

The car itself was a mass of twisted metal. Bits of glass and metal became shrapnel, ripping into fabric on the inside. The roof of the car was bowed upward by the force of the blast. The left front fender and tire were destroyed as the large motor had focused the blast out that side of the vehicle. The blast blew open the car's trunk and knocked off the gas tank below it. One of the Hoards' dogs, along with a neighbor's dog, ran away after the blast, only to return a few days later after the crowds at the scene of the crime had left.

Al Westmoreland was just 19 years old when he got the call from Imogene that tragic morning telling him to "get out to the house fast."

"I remember it like it was yesterday," he said.

Al was the son of Jefferson's police chief, Albert Westmoreland, and Imogene's nephew. The younger Westmoreland was taking summer classes in Gainesville in between his freshman and sophomore years of college. On August 7, 1967, his classes didn't start until late morning and he waited at his parents' house in Jefferson, about three miles from the Hoard's house. He was sitting in the living room when he heard the explosion.

"Back then, it was pretty common to have sonic booms...and I thought that's what it was. I thought it was a jet," he said.

Westmoreland continued lying on the sofa until the phone rang. Imogene was on the other end of the phone. Westmoreland first thought it was a prankster.

"My first reaction was that someone was playing a trick on us," he said. Westmoreland said it was common for the family to receive prank calls. "I almost hung up and then I realized that it was my Aunt Imogene," he said. "She was just screaming."

Westmoreland calmed Imogene down and she instructed him: "Get Horace (Jackson) and get out to the house fast." Westmoreland called Jackson, the local funeral home director and ambulance driver, and told him he wasn't sure what was going on, but it was "something bad." He then called city hall and told them to get in touch with his father.

The younger Westmoreland met Jackson and the two traveled to Hoard's house with the ambulance sirens and lights on. They were traveling about 70 miles per hour, which Westmoreland said was "about as fast as those old ambulances would go." Chief Westmoreland passed them on the road.

When they made it to Hoard's house, Al remembers seeing a large amount of solid, white smoke.

"My first reaction was that the house was on fire," he said. As they pulled up closer, he saw the car. Hoard's body was in the backseat. His cousin, Peggy Jean, was in the backseat trying to do CPR. Cousin Dickey was standing in front of the car with a hose putting water on the motor area. Westmoreland said much of the flame was gone, but smoke remained. Imogene was standing in the door of the house "hysterical."

Westmoreland's father was trying to get Peggy Jean out of the vehicle. It was an emotional scene, even for the police chief, who was an ex-Marine and a "tough" man.

"It was the first time I ever saw my father cry," Westmoreland said.

Jackson took over shortly after that and they covered Hoard's body with a white sheet. Other law enforcement officers, crime lab representatives and neighbors soon made their way to the scene.

It was around lunchtime when they removed Hoard's body from the car, Westmoreland recalled. Officers remained at the residence, searching the car for clues.

"They were there all day," he said.

At one point, Westmoreland said they brought in a wrecker, raised the car and shook it. Crime lab workers used sifters in search of evidence.

"They did end up finding part of the blasting cap and a portion of the serial number," he said.

Westmoreland can't remember how he got back to town later in the day. Many of those details have faded over the years. Still, some are impossible to forget.

"It was a tough time. It really was," he said.

In his book about the murder, "Alone Among the Living," G. Richard "Dickey" Hoard, Floyd's son who was 14 at the time, recalls the minutes after the blast; how he took buckets of water to try and put out the fire in the engine; how he watched his sister try to save their father; and how his police chief uncle arrived distraught at the scene.

"... *As if in a dream I walked toward Albert, who leapt from his car and froze in his tracks. 'God damn!' he shouted. 'God damn!' He pounded his fist into the palm of his hand, tears streaming down his face. 'Who would have done this? God damn! Who would have done this?'*

Another person who vividly remembers that morning is Gus Johnson. Johnson was on that August 1967 grand jury slated to meet the morning Hoard was murdered.

"I was in the bathroom shaving and the phone rang," he recalled. "I was getting ready to go to grand jury, but they said, 'Gus don't bother coming; Fuzzy Hoard has been blown up.'"

Johnson went to the Hoard home a little later.

"I was coaching 8th Grade football and was concerned about Dickey (Hoard's son was on Johnson's team). The car was still smoking..."

Former GBI agent Ronnie Angel, who had worked with Hoard on earlier raids and in prosecuting both bootleggers and car thieves, was also at the Hoard home early that morning. His boss, R. J. Cleghorn of Commerce, had called him shortly after the blast and told him to go to Hoard's house, but didn't tell him what had happened.

"It was eerily quiet," he said of the scene that morning after the bombing. Although there were 50-70 people there, mostly law enforcement officials, nobody was making a sound, he recalled.

Former GBI agent Cecil Callaway was also on the scene.

"When I drove up there were a few people there," he recalled. "... All I remember was chaos."

One photo of the scene that morning shows Hoard's demolished car with the family station wagon in the background, it's hood raised where law enforcement had apparently checked it for another possible bomb.

In the days after the murder, Hoard was remembered by family and community members for his sacrifice.

"He couldn't live," said daughter Peggy Jean in the August 9, 1967 issue of *The Jackson Herald*. "I hadn't thought of their getting him this way... I had thought they'd shoot him. But I wasn't surprised."

Hoard's funeral was held on Tuesday, August 8, at the First United Methodist Church of Jefferson where he had been a Sunday School teacher. In his remarks, the Rev. Robert Ramsey remembered Hoard and called for the community to not let the lawman's death be in vain:

"...he made his decision, he had counted the cost and yesterday he paid the full price," Ramsey said. "As long as there is one shred of decency, as long as truth, honor and love prevail, this state, community and area and each of us shall always owe an immeasurable debt to Fuzzy Hoard. Like a sword piercing our heart, the question that hangs over our heads is: 'Did Floyd Hoard die in vain?'

In a rare front page editorial, *The Jackson Herald* lamented Hoard's death and called on the community to stop turning a blind eye to the corruption in the county:

They killed Floyd Hoard.

Or was it "they"?

Did we in Jackson County by our apathy, our ignorance, our fear, our failure to lend law enforcement and the courts our full-hearted support help create a climate which led to this heinous crime?

If Mr. Hoard had had staunch, unrelenting support from the public, if we had let it be known, time and time again, that we were not going to tolerate these hoodlums in our midst, would Floyd Hoard be alive today? Would they have decided the cost too great in Jackson County and moved on to some softer spot?

It is almost a certainty.

But the past is behind us.

When they put dynamite under Floyd Hoard's car, they put dynamite under Jackson County. In this tragedy, we as a community were jarred to an anger, an awareness, a determination, a unity which we had not before known.

This resolution — so strong in the heat of emotion this week — must not waver. It's time to get tough with hoodlums and gangsters and stay tough. We can no longer be a soft spot where such can find a solace. We can no longer be intimidated.

We have an enemy in Vietnam. But we in Jackson County have another enemy, under our doorstep, and we must not rest until he is rousted and put to flight.

We must serve on juries when called, never shirking for some puny excuse this sacred duty. We must think in terms of maximum penalties, not minimum. We must constantly assure law enforcement officers of our support and let them know that only the best is expected from them as well.

We must, in short, vigorously seize any opportunity that comes our way to make this a better place in which to live and rear our children...

...To make it a place where a child will not have to run out in the wake of an earth-shattering blast and see the mangled body of a father who had tried, too much alone, to make this a decent place in which to live.

The Jackson County Jaycees also weighed in on the murder with a lengthy front page letter in *The Herald* the week following the killing:

"Solicitor Hoard started this job. Are we as citizens of Jackson County going to just say, 'Well, he was doing a good job,' and sit back and try to forget how he died.... Or are we going to carry on, taking up where he left off and finish the job in a way that will indicate to his family and friends that his efforts were not in vain?"

An *Atlanta Constitution* article about the murder concluded with this:

"Around (Hoard's) new office were the tell-tale signs of the life that was snuffed out — the rolled and wrapped carpet that would have covered the front office floor, still naked... two side doors leaning against the wall, coated with primer paint... Mr. Hoard's framed certificate when he was commissioned by Gov. Carl Sanders as the Piedmont Circuit solicitor, leaning in a straight chair waiting to be hung from his office wall."

Hoard was a writer at heart. A story after his death noted that Hoard "had a flair for words and often wrote prose and verse, sometimes on a napkin at Marlowe's Café." N. S. "Buddy" Hayden who had been editor of *The Jackson Herald* in the early 1960s and was associate editor of the *Athens Banner-Herald* at the time of Hoard's murder, wrote that his friend was not just a lawyer, but also "a poet and writer, too."

"He had written hundreds of pages about subjects ranging from swimming holes and little boys to the metaphysical foundations of science," Hayden wrote following Hoard's murder.

In going through his effects looking for clues, the GBI found an essay Hoard had written that talked about the great apathy the community had toward the local crime rackets. The essay was actually an edited version of a newspaper editorial Hoard had written in March 1963 in *The Jackson Herald* following the death of a 22-year-old Jefferson man who had died while fleeing in a high-speed chase from Athens policemen. The Jefferson man was driving a 1961 Ford that had been modified for high speed with three, four-barrel carburetors, similar to what moonshine runners used.

Here is the version of Hoard's "confessional" found after his death:

"If you have ever cringed and shrunk under the excruciating pains of guilt, if you have ever been so ashamed that you wanted to hide and never look another of your fellowmen in the eye again, or if you have ever felt so low about your conduct that the misery of your soul overwhelmed you, then if you have, you will understand just why I must write this confession.

"This, you see, is a confession to murder, not a murder committed by the writer but one committed by several thousands of conspirators. However, this murder was one of the most cruel acts of injustice ever committed against a human being.

"Today a handsome, youthful citizen died. He did not die at the hands of the law who was chasing him, nor did he die at the hands of justice in any manner. On the contrary, he died at the hands of his fellowman, whose duty it was to give him justice.

"You see, we drove, shoved and knocked him to his death. He probably never realized what we were doing to him. To understand the misery that we are all feeling now, you will probably need a history of just how we accomplished this cold-blooded murder.

"The victim was born and in his early years of childhood had the usual happiness and sorrows that come normally in the processes of growing up. In his early youth the victim, through no fault of his own, was cast into constant contact with known racketeers.

"From his early youth until manhood he was constantly associated with known racketeers. He learned all the lessons which the racketeers taught him.

"In the meantime, we were formulating the great conspiracy which led to the victim's murder. We were condoning and endorsing the actions of the known racketeer. We allowed the racketeer to continue his criminal buildup to such an extent that even though confined in prison he was allowed to continue his operation.

"This buildup continued until we reached the point where hundreds of our citizens were so closely connected either directly or indirectly with the criminal element that the hands of the few citizens who opposed the buildup were tied.

....

"We allowed this situation to grow to such an extent that it has become

increasingly difficult to recognize who is directly involved and who is only indirectly involved. We allowed the situation to remain because we did not want to get involved.

"It was no concern of ours as long as it did not touch us directly. But now that the finger of guilt has been pointed at us, we realize that the reason we allowed the situation to grow and to remain was because of fear, fear of physical violence or fear of the loss of property.

"We now realize that the preserver of law and order is courage and that fear and inactivity in the face of threats and growing crime can only lead us to moral decay. We now realize although it is too late to aid the victim, that each inactivity in the face of growing organized crime was a shove toward the murder of our victim, that each time we backed down in the face of threats of violence was pushing and knocking our victim to the scene where his murder would occur.

"We are disgustingly ashamed of our crime. That is why we confess. We want in some way to ease our consciences and to make amend. We have learned our lesson in crime. If you will temper your judgment against us with a degree of mercy, we pledge activity for inactivity, courage for fear, and – sincerely pledge that we will henceforth refrain from lending ourselves to racketeering and murder.

"Please have mercy on us for we will make amends."

12.
The Search For A Killer Begins

Everyone knew that Solicitor General Floyd "Fuzzy" Hoard had made enemies with his crackdown on local bootlegging and car theft gangs since he took office in late 1964. Those groups were the natural suspects in his August 1967 murder, but getting someone to talk from inside those tight-knit criminal enterprises would be difficult.

Georgia Gov. Lester Maddox responded quickly to the murder, sending a large number of Georgia Bureau of Investigation and state revenue agents into Jackson County.

"I have instructed both the GBI and the Department of Revenue agents to intensify the war on crime," he said of his efforts in Jackson County.

Led by Capt. J. E. Carnes of the Georgia Bureau of Investigation, state officials set up their operation in Room 6 of the Crawford W. Long Inn, across the street from *The Jackson Herald* building in downtown Jefferson. GBI agent Ronnie Angel was the key coordinating point man for the case.

Law enforcement leaders quickly speculated that the bombing had been done by a professional, hired killer and that the killer may have been paid up to $15,000 for the job. At the time of Hoard's murder, only one other prosecutor had been killed in the nation in the line of duty and that had happened in 1912. There was little precedent for officials to go on.

In the early days after Hoard's murder, state law enforcement officials cast a wide net that involved several other states. The hunt for the killer led officials first to Danville, W.Va., where in 1966, someone had bombed a solicitor's car there. That solicitor, who had also been prosecuting car thieves, escaped the bombing unharmed. Officials also took fingerprints from two stolen and stripped cars found in the county the night of the murder in hopes that it would lead them to the killer. It didn't.

Even as the hunt moved forward, fear was widespread in the community and the state.

"The fact that Floyd was murdered makes me think that that could happen to me and I'm not aspiring to be a dead hero," said G. Wesley Channell of Winder, the man Gov. Maddox appointed as interim solicitor general after Hoard's murder.

Channell was on vacation in Connecticut when the murder happened and flew back to Georgia after the governor called and asked him to take the slain solicitor general's position.

Channell had a varied background, having attended the U.S. Naval Academy for a time before dropping out to join the Army. He later graduated from Emory Law School and practiced law in Atlanta for a while before going to New York as an assistant vice president of Eastern Airlines. He returned to Georgia in 1962 and worked as an assistant attorney general before going into practice in Winder in 1965 with Rep. James Paris.

Other solicitor generals around the state were also fearful for their lives.

"Somebody's broken the idea and the seed may be planted in some other deranged mind," said Kenneth Goolsby, the head of the Solicitors General Association of Georgia. Superior Court Judge Mark Dunahoo and Sheriff L. G. "Snuffy" Perry were assigned bodyguards.

At the end of August, some law enforcement officials thought they had a major break in the Hoard murder. Seven men had been arrested in South Carolina in a 1966 attempt to bomb the car of an auto parts dealer in Greenville, S.C., a man who had been furnishing information about car thefts to law enforcement officials. Two of those arrested in that case were from Jackson County. (The auto dealer escaped harm in the bombing.) But it turned out there was no connection.

In the following weeks, agents continued to look into a variety of leads, including a bombing incident in Atlanta and the questioning of two inmates who had escaped from the Jackson County Jail shortly after the murder.

For a time after the murder, the GBI stationed agents outside of Arcade's beer stores to watch, and sometimes follow, the bootleggers who purchased goods there. Arcade leaders fought back with political pressure at the state level — they were well-connected in the state — and the practice was stopped for one weekend, but it resumed the following Monday.

As they probed — often checking out leads just to eliminate suspects — officers debated whether they should be looking at the bootlegging rings or the car theft rackets as the source of Hoard's murder.

The *Associated Press* interviewed a local man convicted of car theft. He said that bootleggers would "have to be damn fools" to kill someone and bring attention to their operations.

"The only thing that could do is bring in state officers," he said.

The work of the special task force was intense. Former GBI agent Angel recalls that he arrived in Jefferson on August 7 and didn't go home until Thanksgiving in 1967.

All through the fall of 1967, the hunt for Hoard's killer continued, but with little concrete information. By late October, the special task force for the investigation was closed down and the probe office moved from the Crawford W. Long Inn in Jefferson to the Georgia State Patrol and GBI office in Gainesville. The number of full-time investigators was cut to four.

A bombing in North Carolina that killed a fire department captain was probed by Georgia officials in the fall of 1967. But again, that led to a dead-end for the Hoard murder. During late November, the governor named a suspect in the Hoard killing, a Cumming night club operator who had warrants out of Banks County. But again, it turned out to be wrong after a polygraph test cleared the man of being involved.

During the fall of 1967, finding a bootlegger in Jackson County became difficult. One night in October, agent Angel took a reporter for the *Atlanta Constitution* to eight different bootlegging locations in the county; none would sell the reporter any booze.

While the hunt for Floyd Hoard's killers was the main focus following the murder, there was also another major drama the community was watching. Ten days after the bombing, Jackson County Sheriff L. G. "Snuffy" Perry was kicked off the Hoard investigation by state officials.

Short and stocky, Perry was a gregarious, out-going man who was known for his humor and story-telling. A natural politician, Perry was also a salesman at heart, having sold snuff for 14 years, earning him the nickname "Snuffy."

Perry had run for sheriff in 1960 against incumbent John B. Brooks on a campaign that promised to clean up the county.

"I realize I will be opposed by the bootleggers, money and old political rings," he said in a 1960 political advertisement. But he lost that election to Brooks.

In the spring of 1964, Perry ran again for sheriff, facing three opponents. After the first round, he had a runoff with I. W. Davis, a state revenue agent who had been busting local bootleggers since the 1950s.

But unlike 1960, Perry didn't run on a strong "reform" platform in 1964. A GBI agent later said the sheriff told him that after losing in 1960 by running on a "clean-up-the-county basis," he decided in 1964 to run on a "get-the-vote basis."

In a brutal full-page political advertisement in *The Jackson Herald* just before the 1964 runoff election, Davis pointed out that Perry had been silent on cleaning up the county in contrast to his 1960 campaign. Davis also hinted, not very subtly, that Perry was being supported by the "King-Pin of liquor operations in North Georgia," meaning Pendergrass bootlegger Cliff Park.

Despite those allegations, Perry won the sheriff's seat in 1964 over Davis, taking office in January 1965, a month after Hoard was sworn in as solicitor general of the Piedmont Judicial Circuit.

After Hoard's murder, Perry came under suspicion from the GBI and the governor. Among other things, they were unhappy that Perry had not padlocked Park's Pendergrass bootlegging operations after the May court order Hoard had gotten from Judge Dunahoo. Perry said he had "oral" orders, but not a written one to padlock the Park locations and that it had slipped his mind. Officials were also suspicious that Perry had tipped off Park in advance about the May raid.

After coming under fire for not padlocking Park's operations, Perry finally executed the padlock order, but it was too late to stop the storm building against him. On Friday, August 18, 1967, Gov. Maddox, Attorney General Arthur Bolton, Revenue Commissioner Peyton Haws and a slew of other state law enforcement officials came to Jefferson to meet with Perry. A large crowd waited in town to see the governor, and to see what many expected would be fireworks between the governor and Sheriff Perry.

After landing at the small Jackson County Airport, Gov. Maddox called and asked that a dish of ice cream be ready for him when he arrived for the meeting. The governor and his group then drove directly to the Crawford W. Long Inn and to what was described as "the smoke-filled Room 6." About 30 minutes later, Perry, his family, an attorney and several others walked down the hill from the courthouse to the inn where they went into Room 6 to meet with the governor.

Speculation was rampant that Gov. Maddox would remove Perry from office, but that didn't happen. The governor left the meeting and made a bland statement to reporters, then headed off to see some of the booze at the county jail which had been confiscated in May. He next went to see Hoard's mangled car and then to visit Imogene Hoard. Maddox pledged to "do everything we can do" to find her husband's killers.

The governor and his associates then went to Marlow's Café, the local hangout located next to the Crawford Long Inn, to buy some Cokes before heading back to the airport.

The day after meeting with the governor, Perry turned over to the GBI some of the beer and liquor from the May raids that he had stored on his father's farm in Madison County and at a store in Arcade. Judge Dunahoo had issued Perry an order to produce the missing booze. Perry later claimed the beer was getting wet on a truck it was in, so he stored it elsewhere.

GBI agents said there were a number of "discrepancies" in the inventory of beer and liquor that had been confiscated in the May raids and what Perry turned over to them. The discrepancies weren't that beer was missing, but rather that Perry had turned over more beer to the GBI than had been confiscated in the raids and that some of it had been manufactured after the date of the raid.

One Arcade beer retailer denied he had ever sold Perry any beer, but did admit he loaned the sheriff a truck to haul the beer from that Madison County farm back to Jefferson. On August 19, 1967, the confiscated booze was buried in a pit and run over by a bulldozer at the county's correctional "farm," an event that reportedly took 12 hours to complete.

Despite being ousted from the Hoard case, Perry announced that he would lead his own investigation into the murder. In late August 1967, he and a local state revenue agent raided several bootlegging places in the county, arresting nine people.

Perry also intensified his criticism of the GBI as the weeks dragged on. After the GBI recaptured two Jackson County jail escapees, they were returned to Perry. But Perry claimed that one of the escapees had hidden a gun in some clothing and blasted the GBI for not having searched the escapees thoroughly.

Part of that tension was a turf fight. At the time, the GBI couldn't go into a county to investigate without being invited by the sheriff — except for Jackson County where a governor's order allowed the GBI to come in unannounced.

By mid-October 1967, Perry was under mounting pressure to resign. Wesley Channell, the interim solicitor general, said he would "welcome that eventuality. It would save everybody a lot of trouble and expense." GBI officials also said that Perry's resignation would be "favorable."

Perry's biggest problem was the county grand jury. Although it didn't meet in August because of Hoard's murder, it had been called into session in October 1967. Judge Dunahoo set the tone in his charge to the grand jury:

"I charge you that you take a better look at law enforcement in general in our county. The criminal element carries on a relentless drive to take more power and wealth from the law-abiding citizens. "

Over a two-day period, the grand jury interviewed a number of people, including Perry, about lax law enforcement in the county. Perry said in a public statement that he had "done no wrong."

Former bootlegger Troy Lee Griffith says otherwise.

"He was on Old Man Cliff's (Park) payroll," Griffith said about Perry's role during that time.

The grand jury agreed with that. The jury accused Perry of "colluding with and conspiring with" Park and others in the illegal liquor and beer business. Among other things, it accused Perry of having tipped off Park to Hoard's May raids; of failing to padlock the Park operations after a court order to do so; and of harassing bootleggers who didn't buy supplies from the Park operations.

Jefferson native Gus Johnson was on that grand jury. As a teenager in the 1950s, he had been called before a similar grand jury to testify about having driven a load of boys to Park's Pendergrass bootlegging house.

Now he was on the other side and at age 29, the youngest member of the 1967 Hoard grand jury. He recalled that the group met a lot that fall and they kept their proceedings very quiet. Johnson said the tone of the grand jury meetings was "surprisingly calm."

"More or less, (we recognized) we've got a bad problem and need to do something about it. It was not dramatic, not gnashing of teeth. Pretty calm."

Johnson said that GBI agent Angel did most of the presentations to the grand jury, but was cautious about how much he revealed.

"They did not want nothing out in the local area when we were getting together," he said. "We met a lot at night, but you didn't talk about being on the grand jury."

The grand jury didn't press any criminal charges against Perry, despite the scathing report, and tossed the matter into the lap of Gov. Maddox, who set a hearing date in November for Perry's removal from office.

That hearing wasn't necessary. On October 25, 1967, Perry announced his resignation.

Probate Judge R. H. Griffith searched for a replacement until an election could be held. He first approached Lauren "Bubba" McDonald of Commerce. But McDonald's wife opposed his taking the position during such a dangerous time. McDonald said the GBI told him they needed somebody they could trust to sign the paperwork associated with the Hoard investigation. After McDonald turned down the position, Griffith appointed Dean Bell as interim sheriff.

In December, Jackson County held a historic election to fill Perry's seat. In a runoff vote in early December 1967, Curtis Spence won the sheriff's seat by just one vote — 2,758 to 2,757 over I. W. Davis. A later recount would throw out half of the ballots cast due to how the paper ballots were marked, but Spence still won and took office in late December 1967.

13.

The Arrest & Trials

As the holidays approached in late November 1967, the hunt for Hoard's killers was over just as suddenly as the murder had happened. After a weekend of law enforcement activity just after Thanksgiving, four of the five men who conspired to murder Hoard were in custody and a nation-wide lookout was posted for the fifth, who was on the run.

Both Lloyd Seay and John H. Blackwell were already in jail on other charges. GBI agents went to bootlegger Cliff Park's house in Pendergrass and arrested him without incident. GBI agent Ronnie Angel was one of those who went to arrest Park. He recalled they told Park they had a warrant for his arrest for the murder of Floyd Hoard and that he needed to come with them.

"O.K.," was Park's only comment, Angel said.

Douglas Pinion, Park's associate, was picked up in Jefferson at about the same time as Park's arrest.

Only George Worley was missing, having gone on the run. Former GBI agent Cecil Callaway recalled that he and another agent had been assigned to bring Worley in following the December indictments.

"We sat in Commerce forever across from where George lived and come to find out, he was at a car sale in Macon; someone had tipped him off and he didn't come back home," Callaway said.

The four men in custody were sent out to four different, undisclosed jails to await indictment. Park was reportedly taken to a jail in neighboring Franklin County. On Monday, December 4, 1967, all five were indicted by the Jackson

County Grand Jury for conspiring to murder Hoard. Gus Johnson was one of the grand jury members who signed the indictments:

"One thing I remember (GBI agent) Angel saying was, 'We've got a lot more we could present to you guys, but have we not presented enough to make you think there is a reasonable (case to indict) of what you need? They didn't want more details out."

GBI agent Angel said that despite the lack of hard evidence, Park and his associates were suspects all along. There was an internal debate among agents about whether bootleggers or car thieves were responsible for the murder, but Angel said he always felt like it was the bootleggers.

"I admit, my initial reaction (to Hoard's murder) was liquor people because I'd been so involved in the undercover buys and all of that," Angel said.

Angel had interviewed Pinion, Park's right-hand man, as far back as September 5, 1967, less than a month after the murder.

"He (Park) was on the radar from day one because of the (recent) raids," Angel recalled. "That padlocking thing really busted his bubble. That really took him aside because that wasn't supposed to happen. There was supposed to be a fine, then go on back in business."

Following Hoard's murder, Seay and Blackwell went to Wrightsville in Johnson County to check out setting up a liquor operation with two bootlegging brothers. They returned to Dawson County the following day. Two days later, they returned to Wrightsville and set up a still to make moonshine in the basement of a brick house, a still large enough to produce 70 cases of moonshine a day.

Blackwell and his girlfriend lived in the house while Seay and his wife lived in a mobile home nearby. Friends and family came around to help man the moonshine operation.

On September 21, 1967, a leaking gas-line led to an explosion at the house and officials discovered the illegal operation. Seay was arrested in Laurens County a few days later and a warrant was issued for Blackwell, who was later picked up and held in an Atlanta jail. Seay's wife and Blackwell's girlfriend were also charged in the explosion and arrested. All four were in and out of various jails over the next few weeks.

Meanwhile, Johnson County Sheriff Ronald Attaway got a tip from the bootlegging brothers that Seay and Blackwell had been working with. The brothers had overheard the two talking about the Hoard murder. At one point, Seay asked the brothers to help him kill Blackwell because Blackwell knew something on him that "could put him in the chair." The brothers told Blackwell about Seay's comments and Blackwell then wanted them to help him kill Seay.

After the brothers tipped off Attaway, the sheriff contacted the governor and offered to cut a deal — he'd tell state officials what he knew about the Hoard case in return for the governor giving him political support in the upcoming 1968 elections. Attaway also demanded to get a copy of all the GBI's investigative files in the case going forward. Much to the dismay of the GBI, he was allowed to get their investigative notes, a situation that would later create a lot of friction between Attaway and the GBI.

The GBI had already begun to focus on Seay and Blackwell, interviewing both multiple times. To get to Blackwell, they interviewed his girlfriend, "Tillie." Agent Angel said they interviewed her several times at a motel in Manchester. They found conflicts with her statements and Blackwell's, then went back to Blackwell and Seay and used that to pressure them.

Angel said that one of the key breaking points was when he showed Blackwell photos of Hoard's body.

"He started talking when I showed him a picture of Floyd in that car," Angel said. "I showed him what they had accomplished, what they did. He started talking after that."

Tillie also pressured Blackwell to tell what he knew about the murder. On November 27, 1967, Sheriff Attaway took Tillie (who was described in media reports at the time as a "shapely redhead") to Atlanta where she was allowed to spend an hour alone with Blackwell in a "bedroom-lounge" room at the Fulton County Jail. During that time, she encouraged him to tell everything he knew about the murder.

Blackwell soon confessed to the Hoard murder, at first saying that Seay had planted the bomb. A few days later, he gave another confession saying he had put the dynamite in Hoard's car. Seay then confessed after Blackwell gave his statement. After those two confessions, it was a short line to connect the dots back to Worley, Pinion and Park.

The trials of the five men accused of killing Hoard began January 2, 1968, in the old Jackson County Courthouse in Jefferson. The whitewashed courthouse, built in the 1870s, sits on a hill just above the small downtown, framed by some trees and a small, grass yard. There had been other infamous trials in the old building, like the 1956-58 Foster-Rothschild drama — but no case as big as this one.

A *United Press International* story described the scene in the old court-room:

"It was never a favorite loitering place for reporters who covered the trial or the attorneys for the two sides. Smoking in the courtroom posed a distinct hazard. 'It's a firetrap,' warned Judge Dunahoo in announcing a no-smoking ban.

"Spittoons, filled to the brim with a milk-like disinfectant and giving off a strong odor, were placed at strategic spots around the courtroom. The only real lighting was over the judge's bench and the tables for the opposing sides. A single, naked bulb hanging from a drop-cord furnished the only light in the spectator section. Upstairs in the balcony there was no light at all.

"Old fashioned revolving fans hung down from the ceiling, and because of the 30-foot ceiling, hearing the testimony was a real challenge.

"The huge courthouse bell thundered the time once an hour, effectively drowning out every word the attorneys or witnesses might be saying.

"When the bell pealed only once or twice, the noise was ignored but the judge stopped the trial for the rolling booms that announced such hours as 11 or 12 o'clock.

"Truck traffic on the street outside had a similar effect, forcing a suspension of testimony.

"'Being here is like stepping back in time,' said one Atlanta attorney, looking over the courtroom. "It's like going back to another century.'"

The trials of those charged with Hoard's murder featured a number of heavy-weight lawyers. Prosecuting the five men were Wesley Channell, the Winder lawyer who had been appointed interim solicitor general following Hoard's murder, and Cobb County prosecutor Luther Hames. Channell had asked for outside help for the trials given the size and scope of the accusations. Hames had experience prosecuting this kind of case. He had prosecuted those responsible for the 1964 murder of three Gwinnett County policemen who accidentally stumbled across car thieves stripping a vehicle. The cops had been murdered by the thieves.

Defending Pendergrass bootlegger A. C. "Cliff" Park, the alleged master-mind of Hoard's killing, was James Horace Wood, Hoard's former associate in the Drake murder case of 1956-1958, and Wesley Asinof of Fayette County who had a record of defending bootleggers and nightclub owners. Asinof had long been Park's criminal lawyer and had successfully defended the bootlegger in 1958 on federal moonshine charges.

Defending Douglas Pinion, Park's "bagman" who set up Hoard's murder, was James "Jimmy" Venable of Stone Mountain, a grandson of the James Venable who had been Crawford W. Long's first anesthesia patient in Jefferson in 1842. Jimmy Venable was famous in his own right having been a national leader in the Ku Klux Klan. Just a year before the Hoard murder and trials, Venable had been called to testify before Congress about the KKK. Venable was also involved in the 1958 Foster-Rothschild case. One of Venable's clients was the man who Rothschild had confessed to in jail and he in turn told Venable, who then passed the information along to authorities.

Appointed to defend John H. Blackwell, the man who actually put the dynamite in Hoard's car, was Athens attorney Jim Hudson. In 1964, Hudson had successfully defended three KKK members in the murder of a black soldier, Lemuel Penn, in neighboring Madison County. Hudson was also a longtime friend of Hoard, the two having reportedly met in 1947 when they played college football against each other.

Defending Lloyd G. Seay, the man who pressed Blackwell to plant the bomb, was Gainesville lawyer Everett Brannon. Brannon had helped defend one of those accused in the 1964 murders of the three Gwinnett County policemen.

Defending George I. Worley, the Commerce man who showed Blackwell and Seay where Hoard lived, was attorney Wood (who was also one of Park's lawyers.) At the time of the first trial, Worley was still on the run.

It was a cold Tuesday in early January 1968 when Park's trial began. Among those testifying that first day was Hoard's daughter, Peggy Jean, about the morning of the murder. Her photo, and coverage of the trial, appeared in newspapers all around the nation. Imogene, Hoard's widow, sat stoically at the table of the prosecution in the courtroom as various crime scene experts testified.

It took a week to try Park, during which time an ice storm hit the county, closing schools. Some students attended the trial during their time away from class. Among observers in the courtroom during the trial was a young University of Georgia law student named Roy Barnes from Cobb County. Barnes would later become Governor of Georgia.

Both Seay and Blackwell, co-conspirators in the murder, were key witnesses against Park. They detailed how they bought and placed the dynamite in Hoard's car. An *Associated Press* story of the trial said that during Blackwell's testimony about how he placed the bomb in Hoard's car, "Park, sitting on a gold-colored cushion in a hard-back chair, constantly rubbed his face with his hands as he listened intently."

Seay gave key testimony that he had been hired by Pinion, linking the conspiracy back to Park. It was an indirect link, however, and Park's lawyers would use that "hearsay" testimony to challenge Park's conviction.

A balding, elderly Park, dressed in a dark suit with a white shirt and tie, gave unsworn testimony in his own defense toward the end of the trial:

"Well, ladies and gentlemen of the jury, on August the seventh, when we heard about Mister Hoard's murder, we was greatly shocked, my wife, myself, and my daughter. We all thought lots of Mister Hoard, as my daughter thought lots of him. He filled out her income papers, the first little income paper she had filled, and we all thought lots of him, and it was an awful shock to us, and we regretted it awful bad. But ladies and gentleman of the jury, I didn't have one thing to do with any of it. I don't know anything about it. And I am flatly denying the whole thing, and ladies and gentlemen of the jury, I am not guilty..."

"...And ladies and gentlemen of the jury, God in heaven knows that I didn't have one thing in the world to do with this. I wouldn't have mistreated Mister Hoard or his family in any kind of way. We always been good friends. We never had a cross word. We worked things out. He would sit down and talk with me and work things out. And God in heaven knows that I didn't have one thing in the world to do with it in no form, shape, nor fashion. I give nobody no money. And I had nothing to do with it. And ladies and gentlemen of the jury, I am not guilty."

Park said that he had loaned Hoard $1,000 for a children's clothing store in the 1950s and that Hoard had paid the money back. Park's lawyers also attempted to cast doubt over the case by suggesting to the jury that local car theft hoodlums had more reason to kill Hoard than Park did.

Attorney Wood suggested to the jury that Gov. Lester Maddox was responsible for having Park prosecuted.

"We all know the governor's feeling about alcoholic beverages and miniskirts," Wood said. "Don't let him come down here with his hatchet men and take this county over."

Hoard's former secretary subsequently disputed the idea that Hoard and Park were "friends." She said on the witness stand that she was instructed to always listen in on the conversation when Park came into Hoard's office to do business.

Georgia Bureau of Investigation agents noticed something strange during the Park trial: Defense lawyers had a stack of papers that they would flip through when prosecutors turned their pages. The agents soon figured out that Park's lawyers had copies of all their investigative notes — and the only source for that would have been through Sheriff Ronald Attaway of Johnson County who had demanded the files as a part of a deal to tell what he knew about the case to the state.

The GBI was livid, having never trusted Attaway in the first place. During a recess of the Park trial, Attaway and a GBI agent exchanged heated words over the issue in the courtroom, according to a story in *The Jackson Herald*.

"We made it our business to find out how they got the files," said former GBI agent Ronnie Angel. What they found out was something out of a movie — literally.

According to Angel, two Atlanta private investigators hired by Park's defense team had taken a new Cadillac, put California plates on it, and driven to Wrightsville to meet with Sheriff Attaway. There, the two investigators pretended to be advance men for MGM and said the studio wanted to do a movie about the Hoard murder, with Attaway as the hero. They flattered Attaway and before leaving, asked if he had any notes that would help them write their script. Attaway gave them the GBI investigative files, which were then taken back to Park's lawyers.

Park's trial lasted a week. In his closing argument, Channell told the jury, "It is in your power to determine whether or not Floyd Hoard died in vain, whether his killer will be punished."

After deliberating for just three hours on January 10, 1968, a jury of 11 men and one woman found Park guilty and sentenced him to the electric chair.

Park was "impassive" as the verdict was read. His 22-year-old daughter let out a loud sigh. An article in the *Anderson Independent* described what happened next: "The jury was discharged. Park took his wife by the hand and kissed her cheek. He hugged his daughter, who burst into tears. Then he was quietly led away..."

After Park was convicted, Pinion — the "bagman" who was the go-between Park and Seay — stood trial. Pinion had only a fifth grade education and like the others involved in the murder, had been in and out of jail over the years. Pinion denied having anything to do with Hoard's murder. He said Hoard was a "good friend" who had done some legal work for him when he divorced.

But telephone company executives produced records during the Pinion trial of multiple phone calls between Seay and Pinion and Seay and Worley during the weeks before and after Hoard's murder. Another man who had worked with Park and Pinion in the bootlegging business testified that one time, he tried to steal some money from a bootleg house Park ran. He said Pinion chased him down in some woods and beat him with a shotgun, eventually dragging him back to confront Park.

Venable, Pinion's lawyer, made a loud defense for his client. At one point during Pinion's trial, Venable shouted at prosecutors. Also during Pinion's trial, other drama happened. A 29-year-old Commerce man was overheard making threats toward Judge Mark Dunahoo. Dunahoo interrupted the trial to sentence the man to contempt of court. The man was arrested in the courtroom, taken to jail and released three days later.

As with Park, a jury soon found Pinion guilty and he was sentenced to life in prison.

George Worley, who had been on the run since the indictments, finally turned himself in to the Banks County sheriff the day Park was found guilty. Worley said he had been scared to turn himself in to the GBI and their "shotguns."

The following day, Banks County Sheriff M. L. Harrison brought Worley to Jefferson and turned him over to Jackson County Sheriff Curtis Spence. A photo of the exchange outside the Jackson County Jail shows Worley, a stocky man with a balding forehead, wearing a long, wool coat and clutching a box in his left hand labeled for a vaporizer. Worley isn't handcuffed and is looking off in the distance as the two sheriffs talk.

Within days of his capture, Worley stood trial. Like Park and Pinion, he also testified that he had nothing to do with the murder. He claimed he was at home the night it happened. Worley's trial was interrupted for a short time when four jurors got sick with the flu.

Worley was also found guilty and sentenced to life in prison.

Blackwell and Seay, both of whom had cooperated with prosecutors, plead guilty after the other three trials and were sentenced to life in prison. Blackwell had been promised that recommendation while Seay had not. But prosecutors asked Judge Dunahoo to give Seay the same life sentence because without Seay's testimony, they would not have been able to convict the others.

Even as the trials progressed during January 1968, the bootlegging in Jackson County continued. On Friday night January 12, state revenue agents hit three bootlegging joints in Jackson County and arrested six people, including Aubrey Joe Allen of Commerce. Allen ran a taxi cab service that delivered booze to customers. Two of his drivers were charged and two taxicabs were confiscated in the raids.

By January 24, 1968, the trials and pleas were over, but it was clear that despite Hoard's murder and the uproar that surrounded it, bootlegging had not been stopped in Jackson County.

14.
Why Did Park Do It?

One of the lingering questions is why did bootlegger Cliff Park have Floyd Hoard killed?

Former GBI agent Ronnie Angel believes the padlock order was a major motive that drove Park to murder. A padlock of his operations would put him out of business. Another aspect was that Park was influential in the North Georgia world of bootlegging and had been almost untouchable for decades. But after all those years of wink-wink law enforcement locally, along comes a local man who really does try to shut him down.

"He was a very powerful individual and because of his age he'd been able to do what he wanted to do all his life and felt like he could do anything he wanted," Angel speculated of Park. "I don't think he liked anybody that stood in his way."

That idea is echoed by Barrow County's Billy Stonewall Birt in his book about his hit-man father, Billy Sunday Birt. In a section about the Hoard killing, Stonewall Birt says that Park got "kingpin disease" and that led him to make the erroneous assumption that he was invincible.

Some also think that part of Park's motive for having Hoard killed was that he felt double-crossed. Park had done legal and tax business with Hoard in the past and at one point in the 1950s, Hoard had borrowed money from Park to finance a small business. In addition, some observers believe that Jackson County Sheriff L. G. "Snuffy" Perry, who was close to Park's operations, may have led Park to believe that he had the ability to control or contain Hoard. All of that came crashing down when Hoard raided Park's operations in May 1967.

But didn't Park know that murdering Hoard would bring in outside authorities and would upend his bootlegging empire?

Angel believes Park thought he'd never be connected to the murder. During the investigation, Angel said some information indicated that Park's associate and "bagman" Doug Pinion was supposed to have hired killers from Michigan to murder Hoard, killers far removed from the local area.

"I think Park believed Pinion had gotten somebody out of Michigan and there'd be no way to solve it," Angel said of Park's possible thinking.

Indeed, Park may not have known who did the actual killing until they were all indicted. Sometime in the fall of 1967 before they were arrested, Lloyd Seay ran into Pinion in Dawsonville. Pinion told Seay that "the Old Man was worried and was asking who done it." Pinion said that he had told the "Old Man" that a man from Mississippi and another from Detroit, Mich., had been hired to kill Hoard.

Former bootlegger Troy Lee Griffith said, "when you got so many people involved in killing someone like they did with Floyd, well it's going to come out sooner or later. That was stupid right there with as many people involved in that."

There are other theories about the murder, too. Pinion was the link between Park and Seay, but he apparently never named Park specifically. Seay said Pinion had used the phrase "the Old Man," a phrase which most people understood to be Park.

Early in the investigation, it wasn't clear if the bootleggers had killed Hoard, or if someone in the car theft rings had done the murder. Specifically, A. D. Allen, the "kingpin" of car thefts from Commerce, was a suspect. Even after Park's conviction, some believed that Allen was the real person behind Hoard's killing.

Griffith, who hauled liquor for both Park and Allen during the 1950s and 1960s, said he believes Allen was behind the hit on Hoard. He said that Pinion and Allen were very close.

"Doug Pinion would have done anything in this world for A. D. Allen, they were just like 'that'," he said.

Griffith said Allen was angry because he'd been told Hoard made the statement that, "A. D. Allen would never walk the streets of Jackson County again."

It could be that Allen knew in advance about the plans to murder Hoard. Seay had been asking around about finding someone to do the hit and George Worley, Seay and Pinion were all associated with Allen. They could have leaked the planned killing to him in advance. But there's no evidence that Allen ordered or paid for Hoard's murder.

Afterword

In remarks to the grand jury following the 1968 trials, Superior Court Judge Mark Dunahoo described what Jackson County, and the entire Piedmont Judicial Circuit, had seen:

"In the several weeks of the Hoard murder trials, we saw the very soul of the county lain bare. We witnessed first-hand the monumental consequences of undue influence to secure preferred law enforcement — all the by-products and behind-the-scenes activities of an illicit and illegal dynasty, all the audacity, the boldness, the callousness, the reckless abandon, even the wicked and malignant hearts which it breeds."

It would take many more years for the bootlegging and car thefts to end in Jackson County. Bootlegging continued throughout the 1970s and into the 1980s, although on a smaller scale. Car thefts also continued, but state and federal prosecution of A. D. Allen and his gang in the 1970s eventually forced it to fade away.

In Barrow County, which is also in the Piedmont Judicial Circuit that Floyd Hoard served, the violence continued well into the 1970s. On four occasions in the 1970s, dynamite was used in Barrow as a warning: A Statham beer joint was blown up, as was the Farm Bureau office, the Winder Motel and a Winder policeman's car. Those were linked to the Billy Sunday Birt gang, as were several murders, robberies and other crimes.

In 1984, Stan Evans was elected sheriff of Jackson County amid reports of renewed organized criminal activity, including more bootlegging and the creation of a large cock-fighting operation. As Hoard had done in 1964, Evans ran on a "clean-up the county" campaign and ousted the incumbent. The new sheriff, who grew up less than a mile from the Hoard house, began raiding the remaining 12 bootlegging establishments in early 1985. Four of those closed before the raids and within a few months, the others were gone, too.

There aren't a lot of people left now who remember the tragic murder of Floyd Hoard in 1967. But those who do can look around Jackson County today and see the changes it made over the last five decades. There is still crime, especially with the influx of methamphetamine and prescription drug addiction. And the Piedmont Judicial Circuit has continued to struggle with some of its public officials becoming corrupt. In 1992, a Superior Court judge resigned amid accusations of sexual misconduct. In 2007, the circuit's district attorney, who had held Hoard's seat for over two decades, was convicted on theft charges involving public funds.

But gone are the local gangs of bootleggers.

Gone are the local car theft rings.

Gone are allegations that the county's law enforcement leaders are on the payroll of organized criminal rackets.

Gone is the fear that was at one time pervasive across the county.

Gone is the stigma of Jackson County as a haven for lawlessness.

The top song in the nation the week Hoard was murdered was the mournful, *"A Whiter Shade of Pale"* by Procol Harum with lyrics that seem to describe many people's attitude about the lawlessness in Jackson County before the murder:

"And although my eyes were open
"They might have just as well've been closed"

The death of Floyd "Fuzzy" Hoard opened everyone's eyes. It was impossible to remain willfully blind to the local corruption after that explosion on the morning of August 7, 1967.

Epilogue

• Two weeks after the murder trials ended in January 1968, the Jackson County grand jury indicted former **Sheriff L. G. "Snuffy" Perry** on multiple charges, including bribery involving three Georgia State Patrol officers and a misdemeanor charge of conspiracy involving the American Legion where Cliff Park had gotten his beer. Several witnesses testified at Perry's August 1968 trial that the sheriff had been the go-between for Park in setting up the arrangement for the bootlegger to buy beer from the Negro American Legion Post in Commerce. Three GBI agents and the solicitor general testified that Perry admitted to them he made the arrangements for Park. "The sheriff turned pale, began to heave, went to the bathroom, dashed water on his face, came back and said he did (arrange for Park to buy beer from the American Legion) but he didn't know why," said GBI agent J. E. Carnes. "...Never in my police career had I seen a man crack as bad as he did." Perry testified in his own defense at his two August 1968 trials, saying he was innocent and that the GBI and solicitor general had been out to get him. Two juries found Perry innocent on all charges. After the trials, Perry returned to private life and ran a men's clothing store in Commerce for many years. He died in 2014.

• In April 1968, a **referendum** was held in Jackson County to legalize beer sales in a bid to undermine bootlegging. Despite Hoard's recent death at the hands of bootleggers, it was defeated across the county 1,789-1,481, largely due to opposition from the county's Baptist churches. But a beer referendum did pass in the City of Commerce in April 1968. (The City of Jefferson had previously approved beer and wine sales, but had not issued any permits. The City of Arcade was the only community where beer and wine could be legally purchased before that 1968 vote.) It took another 35 years for the legal sale of beer and wine in unincorporated areas of Jackson County to be approved. It was approved on a 3-2 vote by the board of commissioners in 2003, bypassing a public referendum.

• As a result of the issues raised in the Hoard case, **legislation** was passed in March 1968, to change how the local sheriff, solicitor general and other local public officials were to be paid. Before that legislation, the sheriff and solicitor general were paid largely from fees they got off of City Court fines. Under the 1968 legislation, they were moved to a salary basis.

• **A. D. Allen** got out of prison for the 1963 auto thefts and returned to the criminal world in Jackson County. He was caught selling beer out of his Confederate Corner location in Commerce in the late 1960s. In 1973, he was convicted for leading a large burglary ring that specialized in stealing and fencing clothes. While out on bond for that conviction, he was arrested for kidnapping, car theft and bank robbery in one incident, and larceny, burglary and assault with intent to kill in another incident. He never got out of prison after being convicted in those crimes. According to some reports, Allen "ran" the state prison at Reidsville and was said by officials to be a "model prisoner." In a November 1976 letter to *The Jackson Herald*, Allen wrote: "*You do realize that news media are the ones who made me into 'a notorious crime figure,' and not the court records. There are many people who have been convicted of much more serious crimes than myself in Jackson County that either are not as colorful or don't incur the wrathful frame-up for this publicity by the GBI that we have.*" Allen died in prison.

• Former **Sheriff John B. Brooks** began his jail term in June 1965, but served just one year of his car theft sentence before he was released for medical reasons and placed on probation. The special arrangements were made, the pardon and parole board said, because Brooks had a history of suffering from chronic ulcerative colitis, had a history of several episodes of unconsciousness and also had cerebral thrombosis. Brooks had been serving his term at Stone Mountain Prison Camp rather than Reidsville because officials felt he might be in danger in the larger state prison. In a 1967 interview with the *Atlanta Constitution*, Brooks said, "They double-crossed me to get me" about his conviction. After prison, he bought and sold horses out of his Pendergrass farm. Brooks died in 1978.

• Former Superior Court **Judge Maylon Clinkscales** lost a series of appeals over his 1961 disbarment and returned to private life and his oil company. He and his wife also ran a motel in Panama City Beach, Fla. in the 1960s and 1970s. In the 1980s, he spent time in federal prison over a violation of federal fuel allocation laws. He died in 1989.

• **Troy Lee Griffith,** the former bootlegger who had contact with many of the main players in the Hoard case, had begun bootlegging in the 1950s, making and running moonshine. He said that after being caught in the late

1950s with some moonshine, he was given a choice of jail or join the military. He joined the Army in 1959 and went to Korea. When he got back home, a judge asked him how he'd gotten by with such a large moonshine still. "I said, well by the time you pay the judge down there and paid the sheriff and paid the deputies and you paid the people for making it, there wasn't much left. And he throwed the case out." Griffith was later controversial for a waste oil business that led to an EPA Superfund site, and for a strip club he owned in Arcade in the 1990s. He is now retired and living in Banks County. "I'm in bed every night by 7 o'clock," he said when interviewed for this book. "I don't hang out at these places anymore. Hell, all my friends are dead and I don't know nobody." Griffith's niece, Janis Mangum, was elected sheriff of Jackson County in 2012.

• A **strange footnote** to the events: Sometime following the murder, an auto tag appeared in the Barrow County tag office with just the name "Hoard" on it. It was turned over to the GBI for further investigation.

• The Northeast Georgia area once known for illegal moonshine has since become home to a number of small, **legal distilleries** allowed under new state laws. There are special festivals held in some mountain towns of North Georgia to celebrate the area's moonshining history. Although it's illegal, some in the area continue to make moonshine as a hobby. Prefabricated moonshine stills and accessories are available for order from a variety of on-line dealers.

• Although the Floyd Hoard murder is sometimes linked to the **"Dixie Mafia,"** that's a misnomer. The term "Dixie Mafia" came into use only after Hoard's murder. It was used by law enforcement and the press to describe associations of criminal gangs across the South that reached their peak in the 1970s. In his book, *Rock Solid In His Own Words,"* Billy Stonewall Birt says that after Hoard's murder, his hit-man father, Billy Sunday Birt, organized a meeting of North Georgia underworld leaders at a night club in Athens in a bid to coordinate their response to the "heat" they were feeling from law enforcement in the wake of Hoard's killing. The group agreed that they would not assassinate any more public officials in the area unless they warned the other leaders first. "That was the day that Georgia's first and only 'Dixie Mafia' was born," Stonewall Birt says in his book. Billy Sunday Birt's gang from Barrow County was very active throughout the 1970s, robbing banks and jewelry stores, hauling liquor, bringing illicit pills from Mexico, killing off informants and rivals and engaging in other criminal enterprises. In 1974, the FBI and other agencies spent over two weeks digging and looking for bodies supposedly buried by the "Dixie Mafia" in a "gangland graveyard" along the Mulberry River near the town of Braselton, an event that made national news. They found one body, that of a Barrow County man. The "Dixie Mafia" was never organized as the name suggested and was rather a loose affiliation of criminal groups. The name evolved and is now linked mostly to criminal rackets that operated out of Biloxi, Miss. into the 1990s.

• **GBI agent Ronnie Angel** played a big part in the Hoard story. But the Hoard investigation wouldn't be Angel's last big probe. He later led the investigation into the Alday murders in South Georgia in 1973. In 1974, he was helping transport infamous serial killer Paul Knowles when Knowles attempted to escape from the car. Angel shot Knowles, killing him. Angel later ran unsuccessfully for sheriff in Hall County. He retired from the state in 1996. After several years of traveling across the nation in a motor home, he and his wife settled in Jackson County. Angel is one of the last living participants of the Hoard investigation. Today, he is an avid outdoorsman hiking, biking and rafting all across the country.

• **GBI agent Cecil Callaway** eventually left the GBI and worked for a time with the Banks County Sheriff's Office before working with the state Game and Fish Division. He retired in the early 1980s and lives in Banks County.

• **Sheriff Ronald Attaway** of Johnson County made no secret in 1967 that he thought he should get primary credit for cracking the Hoard case. The GBI and Attaway later argued before a governor's review committee over who should get $10,000 in state reward money. Attaway argued that the two bootlegging brothers in Wrightsville who tipped him off about Seay and Blackwell should get the reward. The brothers eventually did get the money. Attaway strongly opposed the early release of Lloyd Seay from prison and testified in 1975 at Seay's parole hearing. Attaway was controversial in Johnson County and was the subject of multiple civil rights investigations in the 1980s. He died in 1993 at the age of 79.

• **G. Wesley Channell** of Winder, who was named by the governor to replace Hoard following the murder, didn't stay in the position. Channell, who was divorced at the time of the murder trials, announced his engagement in the courtroom during the Hoard trials as his fiancé sat nearby. He did not seek election to the solicitor general's post in 1968 and returned to his private law practice in Winder. He committed suicide some years later.

• **Judge Mark Dunahoo**, who was a central player with Hoard in trying to clean up Jackson County, stayed on the Piedmont Judicial Circuit bench until 1976. In 1978, the Judicial Qualifications Commission found Dunahoo guilty of "willful misconduct in office" over a case unrelated to the Hoard matter. The Georgia Supreme Court subsequently banned Dunahoo from serving as a senior superior court judge. He died in 1983.

• **Luther Hames**, who had helped prosecute the five men involved in the Hoard murder, became a legendary Superior Court judge in Cobb County. He assisted Lloyd Seay's release from prison, remembering how critical Seay's testimony had been in the convictions of those who killed Hoard. Hames died in 1990.

• **Wesley Asinof** was Park's lead defense lawyer and appealed Park's murder conviction multiple times. He later became a municipal court judge for two towns in Fayette County. He died in 2005.

• **James Horace Wood** was kicked off the team defending Cliff Park after the initial 1968 trial. The colorful, white-haired lawyer ran for Hoard's seat as solicitor general in 1968, but lost to Nat Hancock. Wood later became a controversial Jackson County State Court judge where he often told old war stories from the bench (he had been a German prisoner in WWII.) Wood sometimes fell asleep during court, a situation that would leave arguing lawyers baffled. He is remembered for his book about the Foster-Rothschild case of 1956-58 that he and Hoard had worked together on defending Foster. Wood died in 1997.

• Park's daughter, **Diane**, married and left Jackson County. She is now retired and living in Georgia. She has two adult children, including a son named Cliff. *"My heart goes out to the Hoard family,"* she said. *"I don't know that*

I could have survived such a tragedy. Floyd Hoard was a hero and should always be remembered and revered. I'm the daughter so naturally people expect me to say this, but the Clifford Park who raised me, cared for me, and loved me would never and could never have done such a horrendous and dastardly thing. I will believe that to my dying day."

- Hoard's oldest daughter **Peggy Jean** is a retired pharmacist in Athens, Ga.

- Hoard's son **"Dickey" (G. Richard)** is a minister living near Athens. He wrote a book about his father's murder, *"Alone Among The Living,"* which is referenced in this book. He spoke at a memorial event held at the old Jackson County Courthouse on August 7, 2017, the 50th anniversary of his father's murder.

- Hoard's daughter **Claudine** runs an antique and folk art store in Commerce, Ga.

- Hoard's daughter **Vivian** is an attorney in Atlanta, Ga., having followed in her father's footsteps into the law.

- Hoard's widow **Imogene** moved to Athens, Ga., a decade after her husband's murder and worked for the University of Georgia until her retirement. She married Ralph McCants, who died in 2001. She died in August 2018.

- **The house** on Brockton Road outside of Jefferson where Hoard lived and was murdered was rented for a while after the killing and was eventually sold. During the mid-1970s, the large field in front of the house where Floyd Hoard had hit baseballs with his son was used sometimes as a makeshift ballfield on Sunday afternoon for the teens who lived there and their friends. One of the teens who played on the field in the 1970s was Stan Evans, who would later be elected sheriff of Jackson County and finish the crusade against bootleggers that Hoard had begun. The house has since been torn down, but some of the old hardwood trees that stood in front remain. As of this writing, the land is for sale. There is no sign to mark the location for future generations.

- In 1997, a group of citizens from Jackson, Barrow and Banks counties, which make up the Piedmont Judicial Circuit, raised funds and dedicated a

monument to Hoard on the grounds of the old Jackson County Courthouse. It was the idea of Barrow Countian Bobby Brown, who had gone to the Hoard house the day of the bombing in 1967.

- The small town of **Pendergrass** where Cliff Park had his bootlegging empire has remained controversial for reasons other than liquor. Cliff Park's house and bootlegging garage in Pendergrass are now gone, having been torn down many years ago. Ironically, a large package store stands across the road from the old house's location, the town having approved the legal beer, wine and liquor sales.

- The **City of Arcade** is no longer the state's beer capital. The town voted to allow liquor sales in the early 1970s, the first in Jackson County to do so. But state law was eventually changed to prevent the town from levying an artificially low beer and wine tax. Still, the town has remained controversial over the years for various issues, including allegations in the early 2000s that it ran a traffic trap to ensnare motorists on a new 4-lane bypass.

- Jackson County's **population** at the time of Hoard's murder was around 20,000 people. Today it's around 67,000 and rapidly becoming a suburban area to the Metro Atlanta region. The town of Jefferson had only around 1,500 people at the time Hoard lived there. Today, the town's population is over 10,000 and is one of the fastest growing "micropolitans" in the nation. The old courthouse in Jefferson where Hoard practiced law and where the trials of his killers were held is now used as a county museum and visitors' center.

- **Gus Johnson** is the last living member of the 1967 grand jury that indicted the five men convicted of the Hoard murder. He is retired and lives in Jefferson.

- **Lloyd Seay** at first refused to testify against Cliff Park in 1969 at Park's second trial. He later relented and told the court that Park, through a private investigator, had offered to pay him $10,000 and make sure his wife would be "safe" if he didn't testify again. Seay came up for parole a number of times and the Hoard family and several GBI agents supported his early release from prison since he had been one of the key links in resolving the case. In a 1977 interview with the *Atlanta Constitution*, Seay said he was bitter and believed that prosecutors had not lived up to their promise for an early release for testifying against Park in the second trial. He was also upset that Blackwell, Worley and Pinion had reportedly gotten furloughs to go home for short periods of time, but he had not. In 1978, Seay claimed that he had been "set up" by another inmate when some marijuana was found in prison. Seay was eventually released from prison in 1982, only to be sent back in 1985 for a parole violation. He was released again in 1987. One of those involved in Seay's parole was a young legislator named Roy Barnes of Cobb County who had watched some of the 1968 trials and would later become Georgia's governor. In a 2017 letter to the *AJC*, Barnes said that Luther Hames, one of the prosecutors of the five men responsible for Hoard's murder, wanted Seay paroled because of his cooperation in the Hoard case. Hames by that time had become a respected superior court judge in Cobb County. In October, 1991, Seay was shot six times in the chest by a part-time employee of his grading business in Cobb County and died. He was buried in the Dawsonville City Cemetery not far from his famous namesake uncle who had also died violently five decades earlier.

• **John Hyman Blackwell** refused to testify against Cliff Park in 1969 at Park's second trial, invoking the Fifth Amendment. He was released from prison in April, 1983. He died in 2004 at the age of 60 and is buried at Mt. Vernon Baptist Church in Dawson County.

• **George I. Worley** didn't appeal his conviction and was paroled in August 1983. He returned to Jackson County and worked for a time at a local hardware store. He died in 2007 at the age of 80 and is buried in Grey Hill Cemetery in Commerce.

• **Douglas Pinion** was denied a new trial in 1968. He was paroled in December 1983. For a time, he ran a tire store in Jefferson. In March 1987, a truck he was sitting in exploded on Lyle Field Road near Jefferson. It was first thought to be a suicide. An investigation showed that the cab and the clothes on Pinion had been saturated with gas and a gas can was found near the body. But a coroner's jury later ruled it was accidental. He is buried in the Oconee Baptist Church cemetery not far from where he died.

• **A. C. "Cliff" Park** was never executed for ordering Hoard's murder. He appealed and his conviction was overturned on a technicality in May 1968. He was retried and convicted in 1969 a second time and again sentenced to the electric chair. He appealed all the way to the U.S. Supreme Court, but only his death sentence was vacated and he was re-sentenced to life in prison. He appealed again to the 5th Circuit Court of Appeals, which overturned his second conviction. After serving five years in prison, Park was released in 1973 while awaiting further court action and he came home to Pendergrass. While he was in jail, Park had been held in neighboring Athens, where he was given special privileges with a private cell, a lounge chair, a television and a telephone. On January 25, 1975, the 5th Circuit ruling was overturned. He was taken back into custody and remanded to the Colony Prison Farm for aged and infirm inmates in Milledgeville. He died there in 1978. One of those who brought Park's body back home was Stan Evans, who at the time worked at a local funeral home. Evans would be elected Jackson County sheriff six years later, in 1984. Park was entombed in 1978 in polished marble splendor near two stained glass windows in Westview Abby mausoleum in Atlanta where his mother had been buried in 1959.

• **Floyd "Fuzzy" Hoard** is buried on the west side in Woodbine Cemetery in Jefferson. A small, flat, bronze marker with only his name, birth and death dates marks his grave. There is no hint there of the sacrifice he made in 1967.

Sources

Newspapers & Magazines

–The Atlanta Constitution, Atlanta
–The Jackson Herald, Jefferson
–The Winder News, Winder
–The Barrow County News, Winder
–The Commerce News, Commerce
–The Athens-Banner Herald, Athens
–The Southern Banner, Athens
–The Southern Watchman, Athens
–The Gainesville Times, Gainesville
–The Anderson Independent, Anderson S.C.
–The Associated Press
–United Press International
–New York Times
–Christian Index

Books

James H. Wood and John Ross, *Nothing But The Truth* (Garden City, NJ: Doubleday & Company, Inc.: 1960)

G. Richard Hoard, *Alone Among The Living* (University of Georgia Press, Athens, Ga.: 1994)

Daniel S. Pierce, *Real NASCAR White Lightning, Red Clay* (The University of North Carolina Press: 2010)

Michael L. Radelet, Hugo Adam Bedau, Costance E. Putnam, *In Spite of Innocence* (Northeastern University Press, Boston, Mass.: 1992)

Judith Garrison, *North Georgia Moonshine* (American Plate, Charleston, S.C.: 2015)

The Jackson Herald staff, *Our Time and Place* (Self-Published, Jefferson, Ga.: 2000)

Billy Stonewall Birt, *Rock Solid The True Story of Georgia's Dixie Mafia* (Self-Published, Winder, Ga.: 2017)

Billy Stonewall Birt, *Rock Solid The Inside Story of Billy Sunday Birt* (Self-Published, Winder, Ga.: 2017)

Joseph Earl Dabney, *Mountain Spirits* (Bright Mountain Books, Asheville, N.C.: 1974)

Individuals
–Former Georgia Bureau of Investigation Agent Ronnie Angel
–Former GBI Agent Cecil Callaway
–Jefferson native Gus Johnson
–Former bootlegger Troy Lee Griffith
–Al Westmoreland, nephew to Imogene Hoard
–G. Richard "Dickey" Hoard, son of Floyd Hoard
–Former Jackson County Sheriff Stan Evans
–Jefferson native Cecil Buffington
–Jacque Wilkes, retired lawyer
–Jimmy Booth, former editor of *The Jackson Herald*.
–Helen Buffington, retired editor of *The Jackson Herald*
–Lauren "Bubba" McDonald, former state representative.

Other
–Court transcripts of the Hoard murder trials.
–Personal recollection of author Mike Buffington.

Author's Note

The murder of solicitor general Floyd "Fuzzy" Hoard was a formative experience in my life. My parents, Herman and Helen Buffington, bought *The Jackson Herald*, the small weekly newspaper in Jefferson, Ga., in 1965 when I was six years old. I grew up hanging around the newspaper office. Our dinner table talk was always about the events of the day. Although our family had missed the dramatic events that had happened in Jackson County in the 1950s and early 1960s, we heard about the car thefts and bootlegging and my parents covered some of the raids that took place between the summer of 1965 and Hoard's murder in the summer of 1967. But they didn't know just how deep the corruption really ran until the murder happened.

I clearly remember when my mother told me of the bombing on August 7, 1967. My father had gone to the scene to make photos for the newspaper.

I was just eight years old, but the event shook me. Our family went to church with the Hoard family and I was in school with Hoard's children. For months, the Hoard murder was a common topic at the newspaper office and around our dinner table as the events unfolded. For years afterward, our newspaper followed the case and what happened to the five men convicted of the crime.

I was convinced even then that the murder was the result of a community that had become complacent to the corruption happening around it. In reviewing the records for this book, that view has been reinforced. The community had largely excused the bootlegging as just a harmless enterprise in a "dry" county and there was little concern over how the large amount of illegal money from it had corrupted local law enforcement and the courts. Some people were scared, others just didn't care. That conspiracy of silence by the community led to Hoard's murder. My mother pointed to that in a newspaper editorial two days after the bombing:

"If Mr. Hoard had had staunch, unrelenting support from the public, if we had let it be known, time and time again, that we were not going to tolerate these hoodlums in our midst, would Floyd Hoard be alive today?"

One of the threads that came out again and again while doing this research was just how many times Hoard had written about community silence in the face of organized criminal groups and public corruption. In letters, editorials and public comments, Hoard warned about the danger of not standing up to the "rackets" and corrupt public officials. He paid the ultimate price for the community's conspiracy of silence.

Most of what's in this book came from newspaper articles, court records and the books cited on the Sources page. But some of the material is from personal memories. The reference in the Epilogue about the Hoard house where teens played ball in front in the 1970s is from personal experience; I was one of those teens.

I also attended part of the Hoard murder trials. My father had been called as a witness at one point in a motion for a change of venue because of the publicity surrounding the case. During my father's time on the stand, defense attorney Horace Wood questioned him about the large headlines in the newspaper the week of the murder and asked if that was "normal," implying the paper had sensationalized the matter.

"Anytime someone blows up a solicitor general, we'll have that large of headlines," I recall my father saying in response.

In the years after the murder, I came to know some of the key people involved in the events. Wood, for example, became a local judge and I covered his courtroom controversies and re-elections. He could get very angry when a newspaper story called him to task, but he would always calm down and eventually talk to me.

During the 1980s, I frequently talked with former sheriff L. G. "Snuffy" Perry at his men's store in Commerce. He remained interested in county political affairs long after he had exited public life.

I got to know some of those not mentioned in this book, but who were former bootleggers, moonshine runners and otherwise connected to the lawless era of the 1950s and 1960s in Jackson County.

In the 1970s, I attended part of the federal trial in Gainesville where Commerce car theft kingpin A. D. Allen was convicted and finally sent away to prison for good. Although Allen is a footnote to the Hoard murder itself, his auto theft ring and other criminal enterprises had a dramatic impact on Jackson County from the 1950s into the 1970s.

Allen was considered dangerous in that era and people feared him. In one instance, two of Allen's family members — a son and uncle — got into a shootout in the 1970s and both were killed.

My dad got a call from the coroner, so he and I went to a Commerce funeral home late that night. The coroner wanted us to photograph the bodies, so we did. What I noticed is that both men were shot in the heart, an unlikely occurrence. Rumors soon floated that A. D. Allen was really the shooter of one of those killed, but no charges were ever filed.

I was also on hand in 1972 to photograph when officials pulled the body of Carolyne Cooper out of a well in western Jackson County. Cooper was connected to the Billy Sunday Birt gang out of neighboring Barrow County and was one of several area people from Barrow County killed in the 1970s by the Birt gang.

There are a couple of people from the past who merit a special mention for their contributions to the writing of this book.

Two former editors of *The Jackson Herald*, Tom Williams and N. S. "Buddy" Hayden, were crusaders against the bootlegging and car theft gangs in the 1950s-1960s. Williams leased *The Herald* in 1950 and ran it until late 1959. During that time, he mounted a sustained crusade in the newspaper against bootlegging and local government corruption. He was one of the few courageous voices to speak out in public during that time.

Hayden was editor for a short time during the early 1960s and like Williams, he wrote editorials in *The Herald* calling for cleaning up the corruption and lawlessness in Jackson County. In 1962, Hayden won both a state and a national award for his coverage of the bootlegging issue in Jackson County, one of those being for the most "Fearless Editorial."

This book is the result of work from a large number of people over a long period of time, including those two editors whose coverage of the issues leading up to Hoard's murder was indispensable in framing the tone of the community during the 1950s and early 1960s. And the staff of Mainstreet Newspapers contributed greatly to this effort, from helping do research to editing and proofreading copy. A special thanks to Alex Pace who helped research, interview and edit this book and gave invaluable advice on its final structure.

Mike Buffington
Co-Publisher
Mainstreet Newspapers
Jefferson, Ga.

About The Author

Mike Buffington is co-publisher with his brother of Mainstreet Newspapers, Inc. based in Jefferson, Ga. The firm publishes five award-winning weekly newspapers, serving Jackson, Barrow, Banks and Madison counties in Northeast Georgia. Buffington is a past president of the Georgia Press Association and the National Newspaper Association and serves on the board of the International Society of Weekly Newspaper Editors.

In 2007, he wrote a series of investigative stories that led to the arrest and conviction of the district attorney of the Piedmont Judicial Circuit, the seat that had previously been held by Floyd Hoard.

53480396R00091

Made in the USA
Columbia, SC
15 March 2019